SIGNS AND SYMBOLS OF THE SECOND COMING
by
Sean Casteel

This edition Copyright 2014 by Global Communications/Conspiracy Journal

All rights reserved. No part of these manuscripts may be copied or reproduced by any mechanical or digital methods and no exerpts or quotes may be used in any other book or manuscript without permission in writing by the Publisher, Global Communications/Conspiracy Journal, except by a reviewer who may quote brief passages in a review.

Revised Edition

Published in the United States of America By
Global Communications/Conspiracy Journal
Box 753 · New Brunswick, NJ 08903

Staff Members
Timothy G. Beckley, Publisher
Carol Ann Rodriguez, Assistant to the Publisher
Sean Casteel, General Associate Editor
Tim R. Swartz, Graphics and Editorial Consultant
William Kern, Editorial and Art Consultant

Sign Up On The Web For Our Free Weekly Newsletter
and Mail Order Version of Conspiracy Journal
and Bizarre Bazaar
www.ConspiracyJournal.com

Order Hot Line: 1-732-602-3407
PayPal: MrUFO8@hotmail.com

THE MADONNA WITH SAINT GIOVANNIO
In this 15th Century painting a disc-shaped object can be seen clearly as it hovers in the sky above Mother Mary's shoulder. An independent witness appears in the form of a man and his dog who are looking up at the craft. Numerous other paintings from this period contain similar UFOs.

CONTENTS

The End Times Game—v

The Mass Landing Myth And The Arrival Of The Armies Of God—vi

Chapter One—The Second Coming: Hope Of The World—1

Chapter Two—The Soul Takers—4

Chapter Three—Before The Rapture: White Horses, Chariots Of Fire And A Possible Dimensional Shift—15

Chapter Four—A Thief In The Night—26

Chapter Five—The Coming Of A New Teacher—36

Chapter Six—A Return To Spirituality—46

Chapter Seven—Lost In Translation—55

Chapter Eight—A Worldwide Spiritual Awakening—65

Chapter Nine—Signs To Watch For—71

Chapter Ten—The Visitation: Modern Miracles And Signs—76

The End Times Game

By Timothy Green Beckley

Is this it, folks? Are we about to be incinerated when the sun explodes? Crushed to a pulp with the impending arrival of the mysterious Planet X? Nuked by some crazed jihad radical? And if we are about to "meet our maker," does that also mean our maker is about to meet us? The idea of the return of Jesus in what is known as The Rapture is still accepted by a good majority of fundamentalist and orthodox Christians around the world. They believe that there will be signs and symbols in the heavens which will give us advance warning that our Savior is about to come down out of the clouds and save those He deems sufficiently virtuous. Now, of course, many have been waiting expectantly for the return of our Lord, but there is in this day and age an increasingly widespread feeling among the true believers that we stand at the end of time and that some catastrophic event will push us over the edge. Not being among the true believers, we will let our resident Christian scholar, Sean Casteel, take over and show the reader "the way" to salvation. It may be a rough and bumpy ride to the "other side," but, according to the testimony in this book, if you've spent your life doing the right thing, then you may have nothing to worry about. And if you are a New Age-type who accepts the concept of friendly ETs coming to help in the Last Days, there could be a chance you will be "taken up" at the last minute.

Timothy Green Beckley, Publisher
mrufo8@hotmail.com

The Mass Landing Myth
And the Arrival of the Armies of God

There exists a prevailing belief among a great many within the UFO community that there will someday come a "mass landing," a revelation to the entire world of the flying saucer reality we have only seen the briefest hints of so far. We somehow believe we are "owed" a climactic revelation as to the true nature of the flying saucer phenomenon, that we will one day have paid our dues and will receive a payoff in the form of some kind of ultimate truth.

One of the most common ways this idea is expressed is with the phrase "a landing on the White House lawn," which presumes the U.S. president would be the first person the alien presence would want to communicate with. This is sort of an extension of the old 1950s cliché in which the aliens land and say, "Take me to your leader." Perhaps the White House landing myth implies that they have eliminated the middleman/informant and gone straight to what Americans in their national pride would like to assume is the leader of the free world.

Another myth this basic concept incorporates is that of a morally indifferent alien force that wants to talk politics at the White House and eventually be interviewed on CNN. Any number of similar scenarios can be imagined while the waiting for some kind of open disclosure of the alien presence by the UFO occupants themselves continues. We wait, without being able to define what we're waiting for.

But what if we're waiting for the wrong kind of mass landing? What if the UFO occupants are not morally indifferent at all? What if the ancient astronaut interpreters of the phenomenon are right and the aliens are the gods that created us and at least tried to teach mankind a set of moral codes, a system of ethics that reflected their own "alien" morals and ethics? Perhaps the Old Testament word would be "righteousness," and the prophets crying out down through the ages for truth and justice were not merely raving in some kind of sacrosanct psychosis but were, as they claimed, pressed into service as a "mouthpiece" or advocate for God?

There has always been a thin line between madness and genuine religious experience. The story of Abraham and his near-sacrifice of his son Isaac is a frequently used example of this problem. Abraham claims to hear a "voice," which he assumes to be God, telling him to "sacrifice" his son. If Abraham were to walk into a courtroom today and tell a judge his "voices" told him to murder his own child, one would hope he would receive immediate hospitalization. It is typical of the schizophrenic to use what psychiatry would call "religious delusions" to justify any number of violent or otherwise antisocial behaviors.

Yet from childhood we are taught that Abraham was not psychotic and was having a genuine conversation with the true God. We are also taught that God chose at the final instant to take mercy on both Abraham and Isaac, providing a sacrificial animal, seemingly out of nowhere, to substitute for a frightened and confused Isaac. God's real point had been to test Abraham's faith, in a manner appropriate to the historical context of the ancient world.

As UFO believers, we too would like some kind of assurance that we are on the right side of that same thin line. While the morals of this country and the world around us may be said to have deteriorated to a depressing, even dangerous degree, there still exists a kind of social contract, law and order, and an agreed upon effort to maintain a level of ethical behavior we can live with comfortably enough to survive.

We think we know what is right and who among us could somehow trust an invading alien army to tell us different? Would these faceless, unknowable flying saucer occupants necessarily have a moral agenda at all? And should they have such an agenda, would they automatically want to impose that on us or even deign to teach it to us?

What to fear and who to trust about that fear? These kind of unanswerable questions inevitably grow wearisome to even the hardiest of UFO speculators. But this book on UFOs and the Second Coming is an attempt to answer some of those questions by blending the prophecies of the Bible with what little is known of the UFO phenomenon. Admittedly, in the marketplace of truth as it exists today, we already have two strikes against us. We are taking up two sharp sticks of something society has seen numerous examples of in the context of insanity – Biblical prophecy and UFOs – and giving ourselves a painful poke in the eye. Many a maniac with an axe to grind has wrapped himself in one or both of these subjects, usually to nauseating effect.

But nevertheless, we persist in this line of inquiry, of careful painstaking research. I have interviewed a group of experts on the subjects of Biblical prophecy and UFOs. Some have made the leap of faith and believe they are two inseparable parts of an overall whole, while other interviewees quoted here tend to carefully avoid expressing a belief in some future violent apocalypse.

For instance, what does the Second Coming mean to ordained minister Dr. Barry Downing? Downing's impressive academic background in both science and religion, combined with a longtime study of the UFO phenomenon, makes his opinion as "expert" as they come.

Biblical prophecy scholar Gary Stearman discusses how the long awaited Rapture will be timed to events in Israel and explains how UFO waves in that embattled stretch of Earth have always been an expression of God's unfolding plan in the modern world. One must learn to live with the idea that the Day of the Lord will arrive as a "thief in the night," catching the entire world off-guard and entering our reality unannounced.

There are also chapters offering the aforementioned less apocalyptic view of the Second Coming. In interviews with religious and UFO scholar Dr. Brenda Denzler and prophecy researcher G.C. Schellhorn, Christ's return is portrayed as a quieter transformation of humankind's collective consciousness, a kind of moral rebirth taking place on levels too subtle to be readily apparent to the unenlightened observer. What if Christ and the other prophets can achieve their merciful ends without a "blood and guts" confrontation with the wickedness of the world?

The legendary husband and wife team of Brad and Sherry Steiger are interviewed for separate chapters about their beliefs on the Second Coming. Brad recalls his youthful days in Bible class and explains how his views are now less extreme, less black and white, regarding what we mean when we discuss things like the fearful aspects of the Book of Revelation.

Meanwhile, Sherry also feels her childhood religious beliefs and even time spent in a Lutheran seminary as a young woman did not prepare her for the truths she would later discover. What should be emphasized, she believes, is the commonality between all world faiths and the peaceful, good intentions of the prophets who introduced them to us. Yet she concedes she is troubled by portions of Book of Revelation and believes the Mark of the Beast could easily become a reality. Read her chapter in "Signs and Symbols of the Second Coming" to find out why.

Did the late Dr. Frank Stranges correctly identify the Antichrist? He is among the many who have tried to "name names" in that regard, but in this exclusive interview he explains his reasoning for doing so in some detail, while at the same time decrying the "fear mongers" who use the Second Coming to terrify rather than to inspire. Will the UFOs eventually spread the wisdom and grace of Christianity to the entire universe after carrying out the Second Coming on Earth?

Finally, I touch on the possible use of holograms to stage a false Second Coming and offer a checklist of signs to watch for in the countdown to the Day of the Lord, as provided by Gray Stearman.

Returning to the subject that began this chapter, it is my belief that we should not be waiting for a morally indifferent landing on the White House lawn. Should the mass landing come, it will more likely be from the skies over Armageddon, when the UFOs arrive en masse to combat the armies gathered by the Antichrist. Jesus Christ is often thought of as the teacher who cautioned us to turn the other cheek but he also said he came not to bring peace but the sword. In Revelation, Chapter 19, he is called the Word of God, he from whose mouth issues a sharp sword with which he smites the nations. He is accompanied by the "armies of heaven" who follow behind him on white horses. Would you not agree that all that stands in marked contrast to "moral indifference"?

In a book published by Tim Beckley's Inner Light Publications, called "Project World Evacuation," the late contactee, Tuella, lays out in exquisite detail another take on what the Second Coming will include: the promise that some UFOs will assist in the "great exodus" of human souls off this planet. Tuella channeled Ashtar, her name for the alien Space Brother who "spoke" to her and other fellow believers. "You will be hosted by us, fed and housed comfortably in a great mother ship," Ashtar told her. Another Space Brother entity, called Andromeda Rex, even volunteered information about the food: "It will be as nearly normal to your accustomed foods as we can arrange it. It will include some drinks and foods that are new to you, but we are attempting a cuisine that will be favorable to all, with personal choices where needed."

It is comforting to know that the Chosen Ones will be well-fed in outer space, but the most joyous aspect of the great adventure will be "in the mingling of beings from all worlds," when the evacuated earthlings will be introduced to their galaxy and universe.

The exact time of the great evacuation is not known of course, but is contingent on events on Earth. For example, one message given in "Project World Evacuation" declares that, "We will not allow the entire planet to be destroyed. If atomic warfare does become activated, that will be the point of immediate mass evacuation by us of the prepared citizens of the Earth."

Tuella knows her audience. She is not preaching to the masses but rather to a specialized group prepared to understand her.

"Just as many are called but few are chosen," Tuella writes, "likewise, many who read this book will neither understand nor receive the information. But those special souls for whom it is intended will rejoice in its guidance and accept its timely and imperative revelation.

"This information is not entertainment," she continues. "It is comparable to 'sealed orders' given to dedicated volunteers on a strategic mission. It is dispersed to them, compiled for them and will be cherished by them. It is neither defended nor justified. It is data recorded as given and passed on to those for whom it is intended."

There is a vaguely militaristic overtone to some of that passage; the phrases like "sealed orders" and "strategic mission" seem to imply that the Ashtar Command speaking through Tuella is extremely well organized and is definitely playing for keeps. But when you're talking about the rescue and salvation of yourself and your loved ones, who would have it otherwise?

It is unfortunate that Tuella passed away before she could be interviewed for this book because her input would have been fascinating. Her Space Brother contacts have given her a beautiful blueprint for an alien Rapture complete with information on the living arrangements onboard the ships afterward. As a race, we stand on the cusp of Doom and Salvation, and the mysterious, ubiquitous UFOs will be a crucial element of both.

SIGNS AND SYMBOLS OF THE SECOND COMING

The Author, Sean Casteel, at his desk.

CHAPTER ONE

THE SECOND COMING: HOPE OF THE WORLD

Why, after 2000 years, do people still long for the Second Coming of Jesus Christ? Why does the idea of Jesus' return continue to exert such power over his believers?

Along the way to Christ's return, a time of horror and tribulation is often prophesied to happen first. Can the human race truly survive those terrible events, such as the reign of the antichrist, that are said to culminate in the Battle of Armageddon?

What kind of paradise may await those chosen to survive and return with Christ? Is there a form of perfection awaiting the righteous?

There is a part of mankind that never abandons hope, a part that sees life worth living no matter how precarious the collective situation becomes. It is a spark of eternal optimism that is never fully extinguished.

So it is with the belief in the Second Coming. Given the terrible state of decline the world finds itself in, it is only natural that we look to the skies for a deliverer, someone who can wrest mankind from the grip of evil and restore a sense of peace and sanity such as we have not known for many millennia.

But who do we turn to for information on something so basically unknowable? This book is a survey of the opinions of authors and researchers who are deeply immersed in the field of religious and prophetic studies, and can provide educated answers and speculation on the subject.

SIGNS AND SYMBOLS OF THE SECOND COMING

They include Dr. Barry Downing, an ordained minister, who argues that God is likely in no hurry to interfere with the status quo, since it took so long to bring the world to its current level of development.

Gary Stearman, a writer and television personality with the "Prophecy In The News" ministry, believes the Second Coming is being hastened by the establishment in the last century of the national state of Israel.

Dr. Brenda Denzler counters that by declaring the true Second Coming will be so gradual that we may not even notice it has happened.

G.C. Schellhorn asks the question, why must we expect the return of Jesus himself when perhaps a new kind of teacher would suffice?

Renowned paranormal author Brad Steiger says that the Second Coming must happen within the individual person and that an en masse event of the apocalyptic kind is very unlikely.

Steiger's wife Sherry groups belief in the Second Coming with the similar beliefs of North and South American Indian tribes.

And finally, Dr. Frank Stranges prophesies a worldwide spiritual awakening as well as the coming of the Man of Sin, whose number is 666, and whom he is not afraid to call by name.

A common thread running through all the interviewees is that, along with their deeply rooted Biblical faith, they also believe unequivocally that the UFO phenomenon is something real, something that must be confronted by anyone who seeks the truth underlying the scriptures. Innumerable Biblical references to "fiery chariots" and "the clouds of heaven" should make it impossible for even the most traditionalist Christians to ignore the obvious connections between the modern-day flying saucer presence and the signs and miracles of ancient times.

In fact, the UFO phenomenon renders so many miracles of the Bible more plausible, not less so, and should logically be embraced by Christians everywhere. Hopefully this book will help, in some small way, to close some of the gaps that separate more orthodox Christians from the ranks of the UFO faithful.

As Dr. Barry Downing says in these pages, if the government were more honest about the truth behind the UFO phenomenon, then Christians would be lining up in droves to make their own personal religious sense out of it.

The drama and shock of the situation would force some to question their faith, while it would be a deeply stirring confirmation for others.

SIGNS AND SYMBOLS OF THE SECOND COMING

WAS JESUS IN ERROR?

Matthew 16:28 quotes Jesus as saying, "Truly, I say to you, there are some standing here who will not taste death before they see the Son of Man coming in his kingdom."

This passage has troubled New Testament scholars for centuries. What did Jesus mean? Was he somehow mistaken in his understanding of the timeline for his Second Coming? Did he mean something besides that, some kind of elusive reference to a return in the spirit as opposed to the flesh? Or was it an error in translation, mistakenly inserted by later scribes? Since it has not come to pass yet, does that mean we should abandon our hope for a Second Coming?

All of the interviewees for this book were asked those questions. Some responded, and some did not, but the replies of those who did address the issue were varied and meaningful, and provide much food for thought.

One surprising factor that turned up repeatedly in the interviews was how the belief in the Second Coming as a single, historical future event was basically the minority opinion, espoused only by Gary Stearman and Dr. Frank Stranges. For most of the interviewees, there was too big a leap of logic involved in waiting for Doomsday and the return of Jesus in the clouds. But the alternative answers given to that scenario are fascinating in their own right as well.

THE TIMES THEY ARE A-CHANGING

Perhaps, as it has often been said, the only constant is constant change. And admittedly, most recent change has not been for the better. Is it prudent to wish for deliverance, to leave the future in the hands of a loving and benevolent God? Or are we better served to try to seize control and work the evil out of our systems ourselves?

This book cannot answer those questions, but it can give one a background of current thought on the subject, a background one can paint one's own picture of the truth upon.

"I've been aware of the time passing by," singer-songwriter Jackson Browne wrote. "They say in the end, it's the blink of an eye."

That may be more than a clever rhyme. That may be the most fearsome of truths.

SIGNS AND SYMBOLS OF THE SECOND COMING

CHAPTER TWO

THE SOUL TAKERS

Will humanity someday force God's hand, by way of rampant corruption and environmental decline, even nuclear terrorism? Does God intend to use the Second Coming only as a last resort?

Was Christ deceived about the timing of his own Second Coming? Should we continue to wait for a savior who may never come? Or is there some middle ground between the various extremes?

Does the nature of faith require that we remain in the dark about some aspects of God? Would the landing of Jesus on the White House lawn somehow make faith less necessary?

Ordained minister Dr. Barry Downing is a very well-known name in the field of religiously-oriented Ufology. His 1968 book, "The Bible and Flying Saucers," is considered a classic with about 300,000 copies in print.

Downing's credentials as a Presbyterian minister are also very impressive. After earning a degree in physics, he went on to receive a divinity degree from Princeton Theological Seminary, and later earned his Ph.D. from the University of Edinburgh in Scotland, specializing in the relationship between science and religion.

After returning from Scotland, Downing said he began to contemplate the spatial nature of the universe and where theology was at the time.

"And where theology was then," Downing said, "was to doubt that the whole idea of heaven even held water anymore. Once we started thinking in spatial terms and sending up rockets, the whole idea of God being up in the sky kind of died. In fact, the 'Death of God' movement in the 1960s happened just a year before I was

SIGNS AND SYMBOLS OF THE SECOND COMING

ordained. So this kind of stuff was going through my mind."

In the early 1950s, while Downing was still in high school, his father gave him some books by UFO pioneer Donald Keyhoe to read. Meanwhile, Downing had also read the Bible through completely once and then half again by the time he graduated from high school.

"So I had a background in physics and UFOs and the Bible," he said, "and it came together about the time I was finishing my Ph.D. dissertation. I'd been doing the concepts of space and time and the whole issue of eschatology, which includes the Second Coming of Christ as a theological issue. The whole question of angelology is obviously involved if you're going to deal with the Second Coming, and so those were areas of interest.

"Liberals in theology," Downing continued, "tended to see these as mythology, whereas conservatives took them literally. Conservatives still take them literally and don't like the idea that they might be space beings. So my position is not well received by either conservative or liberal Christians. I take things like the parting of the Red Sea too literally for liberals, and I've got technology involved in the parting of the Red Sea, which is a no-no from a conservative point of view. So conservatives see me as heretical and liberals see me as silly."

THE TWO FORMS OF THE SECOND COMING

Having established some personal background on Downing, the interview moved on to address more directly the Second Coming.

"I think there pretty much has to be two forms of the Second Coming," he said. "One form is: what happens when we die? I assume that our bodies decay. We see this, or we have them burned up if we're cremated. In any case, the body ends. What happens to the person? I think that some Near-Death-Experiences give us a clue that there's part of us, another spiritual dimension to us that seems to coexist with our body and is not destroyed by death and goes on to some other form of life.

"One of the possibilities," Downing continued, "is that one of the tasks of UFOs, or the angels, is to collect the souls of people when they die and take them off to another world where they begin the next life that they have. This is not the Second Coming as we usually think of it. But when Jesus says, in John 14, 'I go to prepare a place for you. And if I go and prepare a place, I will come again and take you to be where I am.' For this to be true, I think it has to be true when someone dies. That's probably how it works.

"Likewise, Jesus says to one of the thieves on the cross, 'Today you will be with me in paradise.' So I assume there's a kind of 'coming for us' when we die,

SIGNS AND SYMBOLS OF THE SECOND COMING

and it's kind of like a return of Christ to take us, or at least the return of the angels to take us. But it's not the end of history. Obviously my death or your death is not the end of history."

Downing began to describe the kind of Second Coming that is the end of history.

"From my point of view," Downing said, "God is reluctant to bring down the curtain of history, because the scientific evidence suggests that the universe is about 15 billion years old. Our sun is five billion years old. It took millions of years to get the Earth and human civilization to the point it is now. And life on Earth as we see it now has been planned by God and therefore is serving God's purpose. To bring it to an end, only to have to start over again, either on another planet or on Earth, sometime after a new Ice Age or something, is just, to put it bluntly, a big hassle.

"So if I were God," he said, "having created Earth as it now is, and the human condition as it now is, I wouldn't be anxious to bring it to an end."

FORCING GOD'S HAND

"It may be," Downing explained, "we humans will force God's hand in some sense by blowing the Earth up or blowing ourselves up, so that human history no longer serves God's purpose. If that were true, then I would say that the Second Coming might occur at that point. Certainly if you look at the types of disasters that you read about in the Book of Revelation, they may be hints about the kinds of things that humans could do to cause an ecological breakdown of the Earth."

Downing also cautioned against setting a particular time for the Second Coming to occur, citing verses where Jesus says, "It is not for you to know the times and the seasons the Father has fixed by his own authority," and "Not even the Son knows when the return will happen."

"The angels don't know," Downing said, "and the Son doesn't know. So one of the main warnings I would give is to be extremely careful about setting dates, as some religious Christian leaders have done in the past, predicting when Christ was going to come. There is an evangelist who came to my county and predicted that Jesus was going to return on July 4, 1976, to help America celebrate its 200th Anniversary. This kind of stuff just brings discredit on Christianity because before you know it, you're past the date. Obviously, the guy either was a fraud or a liar or didn't care about making a joke of the Second Coming. That's what I would consider that to be.

"You have to be careful not to go setting dates but at the same time to believe that God is in charge and if God wants the Second Coming to happen tomor-

SIGNS AND SYMBOLS OF THE SECOND COMING

row, that's fine with me. Certainly if God wants to do it, God should have the right to do it."

A TROUBLESOME TEXT

The question was asked regarding Jesus' promise that some of those standing there with him would not taste death before the Coming of the Kingdom of Heaven.

"This is a text that has bothered a lot of Biblical scholars," Downing said, "and I don't know what to make of it. One of the possibilities is to look at it in terms of character. There are parts of the scriptures that refer to the Second Death. I suppose that the Second Death happens when you go in for a Day of Judgment and God says, 'Okay, you're worthless, and you're going to a place where worthless people go.' That would be the Second Death. Or, 'You have failed to live a life that is satisfying to me.' And so you're pretty much consigned to nothingness. You could look at it from a moral point of view rather than an End of Time point of view. If you look at it from a moral point of view, it means I wouldn't taste what death is like until I stand before God and God says, 'You're going to hell.' That would be a taste of death.

"And if I had a nice, successful life going," Downing continued, "all the world's goods, and thought I was quite a good person, and then faced God's judgment and heard God's judgment on me basically say that I'd deceived myself about how good I was, or how worthwhile I was, that would a tasting of death. And I would not have tasted death until I saw the Judgment of Christ coming. So I think that's a possible way to interpret that passage, rather than having it be a prediction that Jesus would return before, say, the Apostle Paul died or Peter died or the other people of their generation."

The alternative to that rather unsettling interpretation is also a little bothersome.

"Obviously," Downing said, "if you think that Jesus meant that he was going to return then, then you have to conclude that Jesus himself was deceived about God's plan or his place in God's plan. And by the way, this particular text contributed to Albert Schweitzer's book, written in 1907 or 1908, entitled 'The Quest for the Historical Jesus.' This was a huge issue, and people were concluding with Schweitzer that Jesus was deceived. Either Jesus was deceived or his disciples were deceived about his Second Coming. Since it hadn't happened by this time, 1900 years later, it was probably not going to happen, and we ought to give up believing in this silly teaching."

The liberal side of the church followed in Schweitzer's direction, and stopped

SIGNS AND SYMBOLS OF THE SECOND COMING

even hoping that the Second Coming would occur.

"And that particular text was the key text," Downing said, "that led them to say either the church was deceived and the church wrote that into the text and not Jesus, or Jesus himself was deceived when he said it, and therefore he didn't know what was going on or he had deluded himself or whatever."

CAN WE TRUST IN GOD?

All of which leads to the question, can we trust in God?

Downing talked about a Biblical passage in which the prophets lie to a foreign king.

"They're inspired by God to lie to the king," he said. "And then another prophet comes along and basically says that God has asked him to lie. The whole issue of how do you know if you can trust God gets right upfront here on this.

"An issue for me that's big," Downing continued, "is the whole concept of faith and why faith is important to God. If you look at the Book of Hebrews, Chapter 11, it's a huge, long chapter just dealing with the fact that the people of God were a people of faith. Abraham went out not knowing where he was going. He had to just trust God. He didn't really see the future clearly. And all the people of the Bible who were heroes trusted God without really seeing the end of the story clearly. The chapter ends by saying that they finished their lives without obtaining the prize, because apart from us, they would not be complete. So again it gives you the idea that until all of human history is finished, the whole nature of the purpose of the church and the purpose of the people of God won't be clear."

THE ROLE OF DOUBTING THOMAS

"Another thing I want you to think about," Downing went on, "is the way in which Jesus appeared to Doubting Thomas. He appeared to the ten disciples first, and they saw him and they believed and then they reported to Thomas that they'd seen the risen Christ. And Thomas said he wouldn't believe unless he saw and touched Jesus with his own hands. Then of course it happened and he believed. And Jesus said, 'Blessed are those who believe who have not seen.'"

Which creates still further complications, according to Downing.

"Notice that when the Second Coming happens," he said, "and Jesus returns with the angels and lands on the White House lawn, or perhaps in the European Union or the Middle East, or however he does it, there's no more doubt now about who Jesus is and what the power of God may be. Just like with Doubting Thomas, once he saw Jesus' hands and touched him, he didn't have grounds for doubting anymore.

SIGNS AND SYMBOLS OF THE SECOND COMING

"The other issue was that now it didn't require faith for him to believe in that Christ. 'Blessed are those who believe who have not seen.' Somehow, you see, it's important to God that we believe in this story or what I call, 'to believe in God's game,' without proof And the problem with the Second Coming of Christ is that the game is over when Christ lands or when the angels return. And therefore faith is not necessary anymore. The faith game is up.

"So when I said it's taken God a long time to set up life on Earth as we have it now and to set up what I call the 'faith game' that we have going — I don't think God's in a hurry to destroy the game. Now, it may be that humanity will force God's hand in some way, by the weapons we've made or the ecological breakdown that we're bringing about. Who knows? But in any case, I just think that God's purpose is to see the extent to which humans can trust God without proof.

"And that's what faith is," Downing said. "Faith is trusting without proof. It doesn't mean that you don't have any evidence, but it means you don't have proof."

THE PLAUSIBLE THROUGH UFOs

Downing made reference to one of many articles he was written for The Mutual UFO Network UFO Journal, entitled "Is UFO Midnight A Possibility?" which appeared in the May 2000 issue.

"What I argued was that one of the roles of UFOs would be to move us to the point where the Biblical faith is more scientifically plausible," Downing said. "You've got a huge split in American culture now between fundamentalists who believe the Bible just because God inspired the Bible and therefore it must be true. Then you have university types who don't see the Bible as different from any other book and pretty much don't believe that God is any part of the universe. They believe the universe was in some sense 'self-created' by ways we don't yet understand and therefore there's no divine force behind anything that we see. Our kids may be brought up in a Christian home and then are shot into this agnostic university system.

"You end up," Downing continued, "with the political split like we've got between Republicans and Democrats now. We've got this kind of schizophrenia, you know. We've got either this kind of fundamentalism that insists on believing with its eyes closed, or you get the atheism of the far left. That's pretty much the dominant force in what we see in American culture.

"So the question is, how do you get faith back in play? Not based on the Bible alone, but based on modern evidence that says, 'Hey, the angels may still be here.' To me, that's where the UFOs come into the scene. Fundamentalist Christians, of course, tend to see UFOs as demonic. The assumption of fundamentalists

SIGNS AND SYMBOLS OF THE SECOND COMING

is that if UFOs were really the angels of God, they'd show themselves openly. Yet, obviously, the angels of God do not show themselves openly to us. Otherwise, we'd all see them. There's some part of God that holds God's self back, that doesn't reveal God directly to us. That's what makes the 'faith game' both necessary and possible."

But Downing said that conservative Christians have a hard time understanding that basic condition of God's efforts to communicate with humanity.

"At the same time," Downing explained, "if God stays too hidden, we won't believe. Nobody wants to believe in a God that doesn't exist. So God has to walk this thin line of revelation whereby God shows Himself enough that belief is possible but at the same time hides enough so that belief is not required. It's a choice you can make. And the argument I made in the MUFON Journal article is that I think God is more likely to use the UFO force to get faith back in business in what you'd call the intellectual side of our culture now, which is very atheistic."

And where does Downing place himself in all that?

"I walk a line," he said, "that's somewhere between where Christian fundamentalists are, who would be the ones most likely to be upfront about believing in the Second Coming, and the liberal elements, who figure that the Second Coming of Jesus is like a Santa Claus story that we'd be better off without."

WHY DOES THE HOPE PERSIST?

In a world torn apart by opposing extremes of blind faith and atheistic materialist thinking, the hope of an almost immediate Second Coming of Christ still persists among some people. But why?

"This gets excitement up," Downing said. "If I knew Jesus was going to be returning tomorrow, or even next week, it would change my view of how I go at things. I probably wouldn't worry about putting the garbage out on Thursday, as I normally do. You change your value system if you think history is coming to an end within two or three days. It sets you free from a lot of anxieties about the future.

"So I think the reason why the hope for the Second Coming stays with us is that we want history to make sense. We want there to be a big plan somewhere up in the sky that somebody made, so that life isn't like Shakespeare says, 'Full of sound and fury and signifying nothing.' The hope of the Second Coming is positive in the sense that it says that somebody is minding the store here, and even though we can't see the person in charge, eventually it will all come out and we'll know what the truth is and what the purpose of our own lives is and what the purpose of human history is. The idea of the Second Coming gives meaning to our

SIGNS AND SYMBOLS OF THE SECOND COMING

struggle. That's why the hope of the Second Coming stays alive.

"Also, anyone would hope that a Day of Judgment is coming when God will undo all the unfair things that may have happened to us or people we care about. So we want justice. The hope of the Second Coming is actually connected to our hope that there is a God who judges fairly and fairness will be established once and for all. I think those things are involved in keeping the hope of the Second Coming alive."

THE TERRORS THAT MAY COME FIRST

The Book of Revelation describes a host of terrors on the Earth that are prophesied to occur before the Second Coming. When asked about that aspect of things, Downing replied, "I don't have a firm opinion on this. It looked like we were well set up for a nuclear disaster, and that therefore we will definitely have the fire next time. Yet that seems to have receded, at least in terms of the press.

"Obviously," he continued, "if terrorists learn how to make nuclear weapons in their basement, why then we may have nuclear terror on our hands, even coming from we know not where. So those kinds of things may still be 'plagues' that are going to be in our near future. I think the population explosion is going to put the resources of the Earth very much on trial, in terms of the ability to sustain human life without plagues. All you have to do is have a pretty major weather interruption, and suddenly your six to eight billion population of the Earth would not be able to sustain life very well.

"Our American economy now is so oil-dependent. You read about it in the paper and everyone says, 'Yeah, I have to pay $2 for gas now. It's terrible.' But the whole American economy has been built around oil. You get in your car, you can drive to McDonald's, you can drive to the store. Half of America I bet doesn't live within walking distance of a grocery market. So we're automobile-dependent, and if they turned off that spigot, what would happen in American life? How would Americans treat each other? What would happen in terms of violence in this country? There are a lot of things that can happen just in the way in which human culture is maintained right now, what we would call our scientific and technological culture, that could blow things up pretty fast. Now, whether or not these things would then lead to the Second Coming of Christ, I don't know."

Why does God feel it necessary to subject us to those kinds of potential horrors?

"I don't like it," Downing answered, "but the fundamental story is that you have to be crucified with Christ before you can be raised with him. It's sort of like until you experience the bad news, you can't appreciate the good news. I wish

SIGNS AND SYMBOLS OF THE SECOND COMING

there were a better way to say it, and I wish it were not true, but that's how it seems to be."

A "STAR WARS" SECOND COMING?

The question was posed to Downing as to whether there is an End Times relationship between UFOs and the Second Coming? Will Jesus be arriving in a UFO? Is the antichrist equipped with his own army of UFOs? Like a sort of "Star Wars" fulfillment of the Second Coming?

"These are tricky things," Downing acknowledged, "and I think it's important to deal with them as best you can in the book. Let's start with the issue of if UFOs carry the angels of God. And I say 'if' because I don't have proof that it's true, but that's a big question that I think our culture needs to be asking. I think that religious people would have been asking it if the government had not lied about it. The religious people have trusted the government too much on this, you know?

"Religious people should have remembered Pharaoh. Pharaoh's not a guy to trust. They should have remembered Pilate and Caesar and these guys. They're not God-friendly people. They may lie to you under some circumstances, so you should stay alert. It just appalls me that religious people have been happy to take the word of the government on this.

"In any case," he continued, "if it should be true that UFOs carry the angels of God as we understand them Biblically, then that would certainly seem to be the way in which the Second Coming would happen. If Jesus was taken up into the sky at his Ascension in a UFO, which is what seems to be said in the Book of Acts, Chapter One, then the other thing that's said in that same chapter is this: 'This Jesus, who was taken up from you into heaven, will come in the same way as you saw him go into heaven.' That's Acts, Chapter One, verse eleven.

"So it seems to me that what's referred to here is some type of a bright object that carried Jesus off into the sky. Actually, it's referred to as a cloud. The cloud then refers to the whole 'pillar of cloud by day and pillar of fire by night' tradition of the Exodus, the major UFO of the Exodus. It also refers to the bright cloud that hovered over Jesus at the Transfiguration in Matthew, Chapter Seventeen, and brought both Moses and Elijah to Jesus at that point. So these clouds provide the heavenly transportation system. If that heavenly transportation system in the Bible is the same as the UFOs that we have now, then that's how Jesus will return with his angels."

In other words, as he departed in a UFO, so will Jesus come back again in a UFO. One begins to see the pattern of how UFOs make miracles plausible, as Down-

SIGNS AND SYMBOLS OF THE SECOND COMING

ing was explaining earlier.

THE POSSIBLE ROLE OF THE ANTICHRIST

There is, as always, the proverbial fly in the ointment, however: the antichrist. Again, Downing said he is unsure about what to think.

"I don't know whether the antichrist is a supernatural power," he said, "that flies around in the skies in a 'Star Wars' fashion and is in a battle with the angels of God. I can't rule it out. I don't like the idea, but it might be true. My own inclination is to think that the antichrist is actually the biological forces of greed and dominance and similar things that we all have in us. Almost animal forces. My theology of sin comes more from studies of etiology and sociobiology, rather than UFOs. Most Christian fundamentalists tend to see the devil and his angels as flying up in the sky, but the main times when UFOs in the Bible are reported, they're all connected to God. They're not connected to the devil."

Downing then moved on to his personal understanding of demonology.

"The demons," he said, "seem to inhabit human bodies when they have a chance, and I don't know of any times when they're actually seen 'live.' Jesus was tempted by the devil in the wilderness, but the devil is never described there. The whole issue of seeing the devil in a bodily form is very, very 'iffy,' compared with angels, who are in such bodily form that, when angels come to visit Abraham in the Book of Genesis, he feeds them. I'm skeptical about the bodily forms of demons and the devil and therefore of the antichrist."

A more mystical, symbolic understanding of the antichrist suits Downing better.

"I'm more inclined to think it's our struggle for dominance," he reasoned, "which is an instinct we share with the animals. If you study the way in which baboon males fight for their territory, and have their own females — the relationship between sexual reproduction and dominance of males over other males in order to have access to females — this kind of thing, in my opinion, is what has carried over to the human race. So when we battle for territory, we don't use horns to fight our enemies, the way animals do. We use nuclear weapons, which is a lot more dangerous.

"But that's where we are," he said. "If the desire is in us to dominate others, instead of giving our lives for each other, as Christ gave his life for us, then the desire to lord it over others, in fact to crucify others, to put ourselves on top, that to me would be the antichrist. The spirit of the antichrist is the spirit of the world. The war in Iraq has been about who can be top dog in Iraq. That's the antichrist. That's the spirit of the world."

SIGNS AND SYMBOLS OF THE SECOND COMING
LIFE AFTER THE SECOND COMING

While Downing resisted apocalyptic, End Times speculation throughout the course of the interview, he did offer a little in the way of imagining what life might be like after the Second Coming.

"There will be no death," he said. "There will be cooperation. You won't therefore have to worry about working to survive. Instead, you can work to the glory of God. I would think that life after the Second Coming would be life with joy and no fear. If I'm right about UFOs basically being the transportation system for the angels, I would also think that we've got travel throughout the universe available.

"Is the angelic world a high-tech world? Not many Christians have ever thought about this. We've always assumed that if the Red Sea parted, it was done by a supernatural power. We've never supposed that it might have been done by some kind of high-tech power. For conservative Christians, this is not what they want to hear because I don't say it's a supernatural act. But then why do we suppose that the angels don't have some kind of advanced technology?

"A lot of our jokes have to do with what kind of car are you going to have when you get to heaven? We don't have any trouble imagining that we can project our own technology into a heavenly world. But why not suppose that the heavenly world has a technology that is way advanced over ours and gives you transportation throughout the universe or into other universes, if there are such? This is highly speculative, but at the same time I think it's the kind of speculation that the Christian Church needs to do. And I think it will emerge if the government starts revealing that UFOs are real and that they apparently are piloted by beings that are in some ways superior to us and have a purpose that includes watching over us in some way."

Downing discussed the concluding chapters of the Book of Revelation in this same high-tech vein.

"It does say that there's no darkness there," he said. "It sounds like you've got a world which operates by something that's an eternal sun. The question then is, can we comprehend this other world even if we're taken into it in some kind of journey? Can we really understand what we're seeing? Could John understand his Revelation vision really? And can we interpret it properly? This is the tricky thing, you know.

"I mean, it's one thing to read a travel brochure on, say, going to Venice," Downing said. "And it's quite a different thing to actually go there. The Book of Revelation is kind of a travel brochure on the future. I'm not sure how much of it we can really figure out until we get there."

SIGNS AND SYMBOLS OF THE SECOND COMING

TV Evangelist Gary Stearman

CHAPTER THREE

BEFORE THE RAPTURE: WHITE HORSES,

CHARIOTS OF FIRE AND A POSSIBLE DIMENSIONAL SHIFT

The "catching away" of the Church could happen at any moment. Are 2000 years of waiting almost over?

Does the re-establishment of the national state of Israel, which many regard as a crucial fulfillment of Biblical prophecy, point the way to the fulfillment of other prophecies, such as a Battle of Armageddon over the skies of Jerusalem?

Will the coming of the New Jerusalem be a kind of real-life science fiction, heralding a kind of paradise totally and completely alien to our world today?

Based in Oklahoma City, Gary Stearman is a leading figure in a ministry called "Prophecy in the News." He hosts a television program seen widely on cable and satellite and publishes a monthly magazine dealing with, as the name implies, the fulfillment of Biblical prophecy in the present day unfolding of news and current events.

SIGNS AND SYMBOLS OF THE SECOND COMING

Stearman has been a professional writer since the 1960s and began to turn to Christian writing in the following decade.

"Interestingly," Stearman said, "I don't hold a theological degree. My degrees are in literary analysis and Shakespearian analysis, all of which has had the unexpected effect of giving me a tremendous basis for Bible study. When I took the college courses that I did, I never realized I'd be using them as a student of the Bible."

After joining the "Prophecy in the News" ministry in 1987, Stearman collaborated with the late Dr. J.R. Church, the former head of the ministry, on several books, including one called "The Mystery of the Menorah and the Hebrew Alphabet."

"It was very groundbreaking," Stearman said, "in terms of what we call 'structural analysis' of the Bible, seeing the Bible as based on a larger outline which is not visible on the surface text."

Stearman's interest in UFOs began in the 1960s, when he had several personal sightings that were part of a larger flap going on at the time.

"That wave of sightings," he said, "was correlated, at least in my opinion, to the Six Day War of June of 1967 in Israel. I've subsequently noted and have written about the subject, the fact that many of the UFO waves seem to be coordinated with events that happen to national Israel. Which, by the way, shouldn't be too surprising, since national Israel is the centerpiece of God's prophetic program.

"I saw a number of UFOs," Stearman continued, "while I was standing with several other witnesses, and this, needless to say, really opened my eyes to a brand new way of thinking. I started studying UFOs and I've been doing so ever since."

STEARMAN AND THE TROUBLESOME VERSES

As with Dr. Barry Downing in the previous chapter, Stearman was asked his opinion on the Bible verses in which Jesus told his followers that some of them would not taste death before the coming of the Kingdom of Heaven.

"I would answer it this way," Steannan replied. "When Jesus uttered those words, he was talking to Peter, James and John. And he said that some of you standing here will not die until you see the Son of Man coming in his Kingdom. Well, that's in Matthew Sixteen. And the very next chapter, Matthew Seventeen, features the Transfiguration, in which Jesus took the disciples up to the mountaintop and they saw Moses and Elijah, and Jesus was transfigured before their eyes.

"So one answer to this question," he said, "about when the Kingdom will

SIGNS AND SYMBOLS OF THE SECOND COMING

come, is that it's already come figuratively at the Transfiguration. It was kind of a preview of the Kingdom."

Which leads Stearman to the second part of his answer.

"If the Transfiguration happened as described in the Bible," he said, "and I believe it did, then it presents us with absolute affirmation that the Kingdom itself will come in due time. That due time has been the subject of much prophetic speculation."

Stearman next began to describe something called "The Year/Day Theory."

"I think at the center of the speculations,'" he said, "about the timing of the Kingdom, is that many people, including Jews, including the First Century apostles, have stated what they call 'The Year/Day Theory,' in which they say that God created the world in six days, and he rested on the seventh. These seven days are symbolic of the coming of seven thousand years of future history. There would be six thousand years during which time the notable events of the Bible transpired, including the lives of Abraham, Moses, David, the prophets, Jesus and then the church. That would take six thousand years, corresponding to the six days of Creation. Then the seventh day would be a thousand year millennium. So that millennium or that Kingdom is foreshadowed by the Creation pattern."

Stearman said that that particular interpretation of the timing of the Kingdom is backed up by some verses from Psalm Ninety.

"Psalm 90 gives the documentation," he said, "for that belief system. It says, and this was written by Moses, Psalm 90, verse four, 'For a thousand years in thy sight are as but yesterday when it is past, and is a watch in the night.' That Psalm goes on to lay out the Millennial/Day theory, in which the seven days laid out in Genesis become seven thousand years of timing of human history, the seventh of those thousands being the millennium. So what we have in the Transfiguration is a preview of the millennium."

LINKS TO THE RAPTURE

Stearman said that the Apostle Paul later expounded the same Year/Day Theory.

"When Paul writes to the church," Stearman said, "he describes a brand new idea to them. That brand new idea is seen in First Thessalonians, Chapter Four, verses 16 and 17: the catching away of the church. 'For the Lord Himself shall descend from heaven, with a shout of the voice of the archangel, with the trump of God. The dead in Christ shall rise first, then we which are alive and remain shall be caught up together with Him in the clouds, to meet the Lord in the air, and so

SIGNS AND SYMBOLS OF THE SECOND COMING

shall we ever be with the Lord.' Now, when Paul wrote that, it was a brand new idea. There had never been expounded the idea that the Lord would take a group of people to heaven, en masse, and in a single event.

"Paul wrote this," Stearman continued, "and to Paul and Paul only is given the full and detailed description of that event. But what's interesting about it is that in Second Thessalonians, he links those seven thousand years to the catching away of the church. In Second Thessalonians, Chapter Two, he says, 'Now we beseech thee, brethren, by the coming of our Lord Jesus, by our gathering together unto him, that ye be not shaken in mind. Be troubled neither by spirit nor by word nor by letter as from us, as that the Day of Christ is at hand.' And the 'Day of Christ' is another name for that seventh thousand-year period. In other words, the millennial day being one thousand years is called various things. Here it's called the Day of Christ. Throughout the Old Testament and in other places in the New Testament, it's called The Day of the Lord.

"It begins with a terrible judgment" Stearman said, "and it culminates with the reestablishment of paradise. Paul makes it very clear that the church will be removed from the world prior to that seventh millennium. And so Bible-believing Christians, that is, the ones who believe this, are called 'Pre-Millennial' because they believe in the pre-millennial catching away of the church."

IT COULD HAPPEN ANY MOMENT

Stearman moved on to discuss something called "the doctrine of iminency."

"Imminency being the idea," Stearman said, "put forth by the apostles, including John, James, Peter and especially Paul, the idea that the Lord could come back for his body of believers, the church, at any moment. The apostles left their followers with the idea that Christ could come at any moment. They did this for one reason: so that believers would live in the constant state of expectancy, which would stimulate them to higher faith. If you stop and think about it, this is a very interesting departure from the Old Testament prophets. The Old Testament prophets spoke literally. They gave timings. In many cases, such as the case with the prophet Ezekiel, the Lord actually gave him numbers of years and days to speak in his prophecies.

"But the New Testament prophecies are always based on the idea of imminency. They're not laid out in terms of years or days, but they're laid out in terms of the imminent return of Christ. And in fact Paul makes a statement in First Thessalonians, Chapter Five, verse one, 'But of the times and seasons, brethren, you have no need that I write unto you, for yourselves know perfectly that the Day of the Lord shall come as a thief in the night. For when they shall say, "Peace and safety," then sudden destruction comes upon them as the travails of a woman with

SIGNS AND SYMBOLS OF THE SECOND COMING

child, and they shall not escape.'"

Stearman also believes the imminent return of Christ and the Rapture are related to events in Israel.

"There was a great man," he said, "a 19th Century statesman and novelist, named Benjamin Disraeli. He was a Jew, actually, baptized into the Anglican Church, and was twice made Prime Minister of England. Once, while he was in Parliament, he was asked if he knew of any infallible proof of God's existence. And the answer he gave is a classic. He said, and I quote, 'The Jew, sir. The Jew.'

"And what he is saying is that the existence of the Jew is the ultimate proof of God's existence. That brings us to the re-gathering of Israel. We mentioned earlier that in the modern era, UFO waves seem to be tied to Israel's entrance into the land and to Israel's wars. This goes all the way back to 1897, which was the year of the first Zionist Congress. It was at this time that Theodore Hertzel and others gathered in Basel, Switzerland, to discuss bringing Israel back as a nation. This event in 1897 actually coincided with the very first UFO wave, which was the appearance of the so-called 'airships.'

"It was exactly fifty years later," Stearman continued, "in 1947, that the United Nations, in a special session, granted Israel the right to proclaim statehood. And wouldn't you know it, in 1947, there was another incredible UFO wave. The 1947 UFO wave is said to be demonstrably the greatest UFO wave of the 20th Century, and included the Roswell Incident and so forth. So when you look at modem prophecy, the number one sign is the Jew and the rebirth of the nation of Israel."

DRIFTED AWAY FROM PROPHECY?

The question remains, however, as to why, after two millennia, do people still have the steadfast faith in Christ's return? According to Stearman, that has not always been the case.

"It's interesting," he said, "that shortly after the death of John, the apostle, which ended the apostolic age right at the end of the First Century, it was not long after that, going into the second, third, fourth and fifth centuries, that teaching drifted away from prophecy. The teaching of the post-apostolic fathers, as they are called, turned to church hierarchy and became preoccupied with establishing a large and authoritative church and became less preoccupied with matters prophetic. It wasn't until about 1000 A.D. that people began to revive the Year/Day Theory and became very, very excited that Jesus might return in 1000 A.D.

"Well, 1000 A.D. came and went," he continued, "and Jesus had not returned, so there was a general cooling off again of the teaching of Bible prophecy. It was not until about 1830, with the teaching of John Nelson Darby, who began to say we

SIGNS AND SYMBOLS OF THE SECOND COMING

must take literally the prophecy that Israel would be reborn as a nation. Darby was the first man to state publicly this principle and to preach it. Others began to follow his lead. At the end of the 19th Century, during the so-called Age of Missionary Activity, when the great missionary movements were established, Darby's teaching had become well-accepted by others. Then, many preachers in England and the United States began to say that Israel would once again be re-founded as a nation.

"Well, there was not even the slightest thought of this happening. Israel had lain dormant for years, millennia actually. Nevertheless, Darby's followers began to preach that Israel could be reborn as a nation, and by the early decades of the 20th Century, this teaching became a standard part of fundamental church doctrine among pre-millennial believers. About the time that Israel became a state, on May 14, 1948, pre-millennialists began to openly teach that we were living in the Last Days as shown by Israel's rebirth, and that the Coming of Jesus couldn't be far behind."

Along with the re-gathering of the Jews in modern Israel, Stearman pointed out another fairly recent phenomenon: the large number of bestselling books on the subject of the End Times.

"Probably, other than the Bible itself," Stearman said, "the bestseller in history was Hal Lindsey's book, 'The Late, Great Planet Earth,' which espoused the idea that since national Israel had been reborn, the Second Coming of Christ would follow soon after. There have been literally dozens of other similar books that have sold in the hundreds of thousands if not millions of copies. All made possible by one thing — Israel's existence as a nation."

TWO FORMS OF RE-GATHERING

"The Bible speaks of two re-gatherings of Israel," Stearman continued. "The first one is a re-gathering of Israel in unbelief, in which the people would come back as a political measure, that is, to preserve their lives politically. The Jews, after World War II, were openly stating, 'We must become a nation in order to stand up for ourselves politically, because if we don't, nobody else ever will.'

"And the Bible also predicts a second re-gathering of Israel in belief. So, those who are watching these events develop believe that Israel has first been gathered in unbelief — that is to say, there's no temple. There is no active priesthood. The accoutrements of national Israel's religious activity are still dormant. The Bible tells us they will remain dormant until the church is taken out of the way, physically removed from the Earth, allowing Israel then to move to the center of the prophetic timeline."

SIGNS AND SYMBOLS OF THE SECOND COMING
EVENTS PRECEDING CHRIST'S RETURN

Along with the re-gathering of Israel, Stearman pointed to other events that the Bible says must precede Christ's return, using the Book of Revelation as a guide. He spoke of the first six of the famous "Seven Seals" and their dire impact on the future world.

"The first seal," Stearman said, "exposes the antichrist. The second seal is the seal that begins a global war. The third seal represents an economy that's completely and utterly destroyed. The fourth seal represents a siege of death by pestilence. The fifth seal is the seal of those souls who are martyred. And the sixth seal is the beginning of divine judgment.

"The Book of Revelation has the antichrist being revealed as a world leader along with a global conflagration in which billions of people die. No one knows when this is going to happen, but it will happen — that is, relatively in time. Christ returns in Revelation, Chapter 19, and is received at last by national Israel. They failed to receive him on his first coming. Revelation 19:11 says, 'I saw heaven opened, and behold a white horse. He that sat upon him was called Faithful and True, and in righteousness he does judge and make war.'"

But let's backtrack a moment. Why are horrors like the antichrist and global warfare scheduled to precede the long awaited Second Coming?

"The horrors of the Tribulation are monstrous indeed," Stearman replied. "What you have in Revelation 6:8, 'Power was given to them over the fourth part of the Earth to kill with the sword and with hunger and with death and with the beasts of the Earth.' That would be about one and a quarter billion people, if a quarter of the Earth's population died. We have in Revelation, Chapter Eight, a third of the remainder of the Earth's population dying. Some have suggested that of the six billion people now on Planet Earth, perhaps only one and a half billion or so people would be left after these conflagrations.

"The question is, why does this have to happen concurrent with the raising again of Israel to power? The reason is that there are two functions of the Lord in the Book of Revelation. One function is to chastise Israel and to expose to national Israel all the wrongs that they have ever done. They were supposed to have been the nation that God held as an example for other nations. The second function is to judge all those nations that have attempted down through the last 5000 years or so to destroy Israel.

"From the time of Abraham to the present," Stearman continued, "there have been numerous attempts to annihilate the Jews. The Persians, under Ahasuerus, attempted to destroy the Jews. That's the story in the Book of Esther. The

SIGNS AND SYMBOLS OF THE SECOND COMING

Babylonians attempted to destroy the Jews under Nebuchadnezzar. Multiple attempts have been made. Antiochus Epiphanes, the Selucid leader, attempted in 167 B.C. to destroy the Jews. The Romans attempted to destroy the Jews in 70 A.D. And right up to the present day, in which Hitler and his group attempted to destroy the Jews. It's been a truism among Gentile world leaders that Israel must die.

"And in recompense for all of these assassination attempts, the Lord is going to judge the Gentiles in a way that was prophesied all the way through the Old Testament. The larger population of the world does not believe that this judgment will take place literally. Those who read the Bible literally, who are pre-millennialists, who believe that we are living in the time before the millennium, believe that these judgments are literal and that God has a good reason for the judgments, namely recompense and vengeance for all the assassination attempts ever made on national Israel."

STEARMAN ON UFOs

After that fascinating but dark look at the coming wrath of God, the subject of UFOs again presented itself. Stearman was asked how the UFO phenomenon relates to the Second Coming.

"People who read the Bible," he answered, "believe in the literal existence of angels, that angels come and go, day by day, in our world, but they are not seen in general. They have some sort of an ability to be present without revealing themselves to human eyes.

"And in Second Kings, Chapter Six, there's a wonderful example of that in which the prophet Elisha went out with his servant, and they were camped out. It was a time when the Syrian army was coming against Israel. They woke up the next morning, and Elisha and his servant discovered themselves to be surrounded by the Syrian army. And the servant said, 'What in the world are we going to do?' Then Elisha prayed and said, 'Lord, I pray thee, open his eyes that he may see.' The Lord opened the eyes of the young man and he saw, and behold, the mountain was full of horses and chariots of fire round about Elisha. In other words, these chariots of fire are the way the Bible describes what I regard as UFOs.

"If a chariot of fire makes itself visible," Stearman explained, "such as the time when the prophet Elijah was taken to heaven in a chariot of fire, or in the first chapter of Ezekiel, when a chariot of fire came across the plain and landed right in front of Ezekiel, when these chariots of fire become manifest, they resemble nothing quite so much as what we call UFOs in the modern era. The servant of Elisha was simply allowed to see these fiery chariots, which means they're not far distant from us. There is perhaps a dimensional shift that allows them to conceal them-

SIGNS AND SYMBOLS OF THE SECOND COMING

selves."

The conversation returned to the verse from Revelation 19 about Jesus appearing on a white horse and leading the armies of heaven.

"I don't believe Jesus will be riding a white horse as we think of a white horse," Stearman said, "because all through the Bible, horses and chariots are the figures used to describe these celestial transportation vehicles. Jesus is said to lead a heavenly army in verse 14 of that same chapter of Revelation. 'And the armies which were in heaven followed him upon white horses.' I don't believe those were literal white horses. I think they are some sort of celestial transportation vehicle that if they could be rendered visible to the eyes of most people on Earth today, those people would say, 'There goes a UFO.'"

In a manner similar to Dr. Barry Downing's remarks, Stearman argued that the method by which Jesus ascended into heaven in the early pages of the Book of Acts will likely be the same method by which he returns. Stearman quoted Acts One, verses 9-11, saying, "And when he had spoken these things, while they beheld he was taken up and a cloud received him out of their sight. And while they looked steadfastly toward heaven as he went up, behold, two men stood by them in white apparel, which also said, 'You men of Galilee, why stand you gazing into heaven? This same Jesus which is taken from you unto heaven shall so come in a like manner as you have seen him go into heaven.'"

"Here we see a couple of angels," Stearman said, "describing to the apostles that Jesus would come in the same way that he left. The way he left is that a cloud received him up, and that cloud departed. I take it that this cloud was some form of celestial transportation vehicle. Therefore, that white horse that we see him riding must be the same sort of vehicle as the cloud into which he was received. So, to me, that explains much of what modern man sees when he is looking at UFOs. He's really seeing a glimpse of the spirit world when he sees the UFO."

WILL THE ANTICHRIST ALSO HAVE A UFO?

Stearman next gamely tackled the question of whether the antichrist is similarly equipped with a UFO.

"The antichrist," he said, "as described in Revelation 13: 11-18, has the ability to display supernatural power. And in Revelation 13:13, it says, 'He doeth great wonders, so that he makes fire to come down from heaven on the Earth in the sight of man.' Now, you can interpret that in many ways, but one of the ways that it's most often interpreted is that some sort of celestial display will be brought down from heaven to Earth. I take that to mean a dimensional change of some sort, that something from beyond human sight, perhaps just beyond the barriers of our

SIGNS AND SYMBOLS OF THE SECOND COMING

dimension, is brought into this dimension and made visible to the people of the Earth. That could be fire. It could be a fiery chariot.

"Therefore, I think by inference, that the antichrist will receive much of the power of these fiery chariots that have been seen down through the ages. Many of these fiery chariots are attributed to dark forces. Many are attributed to angelic forces. That is seen in Revelation, Chapter Twelve, verse seven. 'There was a war in heaven. Michael and his angels fought against the dragon, and the dragon fought, and his angels.' That speaks of an aerial battle. I think that to a certain extent that is going on today. And it involves the celestial transportation vehicles we've been talking about, which at times become visible and at other times remain veiled beyond the dimensional wall so that they can't readily be seen.

"But the antichrist has this power to call down fire from heaven. It probably means that he has the ability to call into this dimension the fiery chariots to do his work."

NOTHING IN THE PRESENT WORLD

When Stearman was asked if he could point to anything in the here and now that might offer a foretaste of a post-Second Coming paradise, he said, "There is nothing in the present world that suggests the kind of perfection that's promised in the Kingdom Age. The only clues we have are the very few allusions to paradise that we have in the account of Adam and Eve. We know that their Earth was perfect in its climate. Its weather was very mild. The distribution of moisture was perfect. The distribution of solar radiation was perfect. Many say that the Earth, instead of being tilted on its axis, was revolving on a zero-degree plane relative to the sun, meaning that the seasons were constant.

"Unlike today, with the twenty-three and a half degree tilt of Planet Earth, with which we have the changing seasons. These seasons changing bring about ensuing weather violence of all kinds, tornadoes, hurricanes, etc."

Stearman quoted from the Book of Isaiah, Chapter 24, verse 19: "The Earth is utterly broken down. The Earth is clean dissolved. The Earth is moved exceedingly. The Earth shall reel to and fro like a drunkard, shall be removed like a cottage, and the transgressions thereof shall be heavy upon it, and it shall fall and not rise again. It shall come to pass in that day that the Lord will punish the host of the High Ones that are on high, and the kings of the Earth upon the Earth."

According to Stearman, "This is clearly speaking of that period in the Day of the Lord when the nations will be judged, but notice that the Earth is said to reel to and fro like a drunkard. Many people have said that this is the process of returning the world back to its ninety-degree position relative to the plane of the eclip-

SIGNS AND SYMBOLS OF THE SECOND COMING

tic, and the weather once again will return to perfection. And let's face it, if you can have perfect weather and the atmosphere of the Earth is restored, that's half the battle right there."

There are also predictions in Isaiah Chapter 65 that imply to Stearman a perfect society.

"No more shall there be in it an infant," Stearman read aloud, "that lives but a few days, nor an old man that hath not filled his days, for the child shall die a hundred years old, but the sinner being a hundred years old shall be accursed."

"In other words," Stearman said, "people will live to great old ages and their labor will not be in vain. In the classic passage in Isaiah, 65:25, it says, 'The wolf and the lamb shall feed together, the lion shall eat straw like the bullock, dust shall be the serpent's meat, and they shall not hurt or destroy in all my holy mountain, says the Lord.' So you'll have a restored Earth. The kingdom and the throne of God will be in Jerusalem, physically. The weather will be back in balance, and health will be restored, and people will live to a very great age, as they did prior to the Flood and the destruction of the Earth the first time. And finally there will be domestic peace and peace in the animal kingdom — the wolf and the lamb shall feed together and so forth. With that domestic peace, you'll have a perfect Earth."

A SCIENCE FICTION PARADISE

The discussion returned to the Book of Revelation, this time focusing on Chapter Twenty-One and what seems like a future technological paradise.

"Chapter Twenty-One takes place," Stearman said, "after the creation of a new heaven and a new Earth in the far future. If there is a place in the Bible that reads like science fiction — although it's not fiction, it's fact — it's the place where we find apparently a huge city orbiting around the restored Earth and called the New Jerusalem. It's going to be fifteen hundred miles on a side, which is a very large orbiting body, more like the moon in size. And this is said to be the home of the saints forever. But the world will also be perfected during that time, and that perfection will apparently include breathtaking constructions. We see things built out of some sort of gold that's as transparent as glass. I can't even imagine what that's going to be like.

"You can see things fabricated out of materials," Stearman continued, "that we don't use for building right now, like emerald and diamond and sapphire. If you could take a motion picture of this place and bring it back, people would think they were watching science fiction. An absolutely marvelous world to come. Totally regulated, completely peaceful, wars having been ended, and the source of evil having been at last judged and put away."

SIGNS AND SYMBOLS OF THE SECOND COMING

CHAPTER FOUR

A THIEF IN THE NIGHT

What if the Second Coming was achieved through such a slow, gradual process that we never quite realized it was happening? Is the expectation, cherished by many, that we will one day awaken to find the government of Christ already in place an unrealistic one?

What if the aliens came and saw that our religious expectations might unfairly color our perception of their arrival? Are they taking pains to avoid being misconstrued as the return of Jesus or, even worse, the appearance of the antichrist?

What makes religion a tool for evil? When do faith and obedience become signs of surrender to a malevolent and corrupt religious leadership? Is there such a thing as a holy war?

Dr. Brenda Denzler holds a Ph.D. in Religious Studies from Duke University. But back in her early adolescent years, she was far removed from the shelter of academia.

"At the age of fourteen," Denzler said, "I went into a fundamentalist Bible cult which basically taught that the Second Coming was going to be pretty quick. I thought I would just barely be an adult by the time Christ returned. Those were my expectations. The group and I parted ways when I was 29, which means I was in it for fifteen years.

"At that point," she continued, "I went back to college to get a nice, handy four-year degree so that I could be something other than a secretary. I didn't par-

SIGNS AND SYMBOLS OF THE SECOND COMING

ticularly like the secretarial work I was doing. And the classes that I really, really loved were my religious study classes. So I ultimately decided to get a degree in religion, but you can't really do much with a four-year degree in religious studies, so that meant I had to go to graduate school.'"

Denzler finished her doctorate at Duke in 1998, specializing in something she phrased as "Centers and Peripheries."

"That's not the way they divide up the discipline of religious studies," she said, "so you're not going to see that reflected in any transcript. But what fascinates me to this day is, what is considered normal? What's considered orthodox? What's considered mainstream? And what's not? What are the grounds for it not being orthodox or mainstream? Is that a good thing, or a bad thing, or kind of an indifferent thing? How does that affect the relationship of an organization to its peers? How close to the mainstream it is versus how unorthodox it is.

"So that's what I looked at," she said, "all through my studies. That was where the concentration of my energies went. When it came time to write the dissertation, I wrote about the UFOs and alien abduction movement because that is a definite manifestation of ideas that are peripheral to the society at large. I was very interested in the way people in that community used science or used religion as an explanatory framework for trying to understand the experiences that they said they'd had."

Denzler wrote a book based on her research at Duke called "The Lure of the Edge: Scientific Passions, Religious Beliefs and the Pursuit of UFOs," published by the University of California Press in 2001.

"That would be the most significant thing I've had published to date," she said. "I'm working on a few other things, but that'll do the job for now."

SLOW TRAIN COMING

Denzler's current attitudes regarding the Second Coming are certainly much different than when she was a member of the fundamentalist cult mentioned at the start of this chapter.

"My feeling is that when Jesus said that it would come 'as a thief in the night,'" she said, "he wasn't just a-woofing. I have sincere doubts that it's going to be the kind of event where everyone around the world is going to wake up — you know, one day we wake up and we have the government of Israel and the government of the United States and the government of South Africa. And the next day we wake up and we have the government of Christ. I don't think it's going to be quite that obvious or quite that sudden.

SIGNS AND SYMBOLS OF THE SECOND COMING

"As a matter of fact," Denzler continued, "any kind of simple, literal understanding of the Second Coming doesn't seem reasonable or likely to me. It's not that I don't sympathize with the people who hold a very simple, straightforward understanding of the idea, because I myself was one of them for many years. But I just have my doubts at this point in time that the Second Coming is to be taken that literally, that tangibly."

Denzler compared the idea of the Second Coming to the narrative of human origins found in the Book of Genesis.

"We speak of a time when everything was wonderful," she said. "Everything was rosy. Everything was idyllic. We were in the Garden of Eden and everything was perfect. There was no sickness, no death, no suffering. There was no struggle for survival. It was a perfect existence. And that is what the idea of the Second Coming speaks to. It speaks to the human return to a condition of idyllic existence, of perfect conditions, where there is justice in the world, there is no more sorrow, no more pain. When everything is in the end as it was in the beginning. What religious scholars call 'The Myth of Eternal Return,' that we will return again to that place where humanity began, which is the place where it's all good."

DENZLER RESPONDS TO THE TROUBLESOME VERSES

Everyone interviewed for this book was asked their thoughts on the verses from Matthew Sixteen in which Jesus promises that some of those standing there with him would not taste death before the coming of the Kingdom of Heaven. Denzler's response reflected her learned background.

"New Testament scholars point out," she said, "that if you're going to take that in a very literal fashion, then quite certainly it did not come to pass. In fact, the earliest Christian Church, the first generation Christians, many of them lived in the frame of mind where they were expecting in many ways a very literal return of Christ before that first generation of converts died. And as that generation passed away, and subsequent generations, people who were born into this new religious movement called Christianity, as this second wave of Christians began to be numerically dominant in the church, and the first wave passed away, there was a real kind of crisis of faith, of 'What does this mean? What does this mean for the faith that we had? Jesus was the Messiah, wasn't he?'

"So there was a very literal expectation on the part of the early Christians, one that was not fulfilled in the literal return of Christ in the way that everyone expected. On the other hand, sometimes when your simple, literal expectations are thwarted, and you have held them honestly and sincerely and deeply, it can, under the best circumstances, throw you into a very reflective, contemplative mode where you start to think, 'Well, what is the basis of my faith? What is the point

SIGNS AND SYMBOLS OF THE SECOND COMING

around which it revolves? Is it in this literal, physical event, or is it in something that stands outside the march of time? Is my faith based in something that stands out of the contingencies of everyday history? And if my faith is based in something that is more enduring than the march of temporal history, maybe that's really where it's at."

In other words, early Christians had to deal with the disappointment surrounding Christ's failure to return by digging a little deeper into just what their faith was grounded in — a possible future supernatural apocalyptic event or an abiding love of God and one another not dependent on a miracle for it to endure.

"And with the march of temporal events," Denzler said, "things come and things go, and sometimes things are really good and sometimes things are really very bad. But the enduring center of my faith doesn't depend on the contingent events of history. I think that is what a 'hope deferred' can do for a person under the best circumstances. Under the worst of circumstances, it can destroy one's faith. Someone can say, 'Well, it's all a bunch of hooey. All religion is a bunch of hooey.' And totally throw faith overboard.

"I know people in my old religious group," she continued, "who did precisely that, who just had trouble and began questioning. They questioned everything, which is fine. Questioning everything is in fact pretty darn healthy to do once in a while. But they had nothing to show for it, in the end. They couldn't come up with any other kind of faith position. It had to be kind of a literal understanding or nothing. They chose nothing when the literal understanding that they did have didn't work out. That's what can happen on the downside, in the not-the-best-case scenario."

Denzler laid out a different concept for the Second Coming, one that doesn't involve a literal, supernatural rending of the cosmos.

"There are different understandings of Christ's return," she said. "Most people believe that it's going to get unimaginably horrible, and just when you thought it couldn't get any worse, finally Christ will return and make it all better.

"A minority view," she continued, "is just the opposite. It is that the power of the Christian faith will so overwhelm the world and turn people's hearts, that the world will get worse and worse until it is finally swayed by sheer force of persuasion, by the sheer goodness of the Holy Spirit and the Christian message. It will be swayed to a Christ-oriented way. And when the world has changed its ways and begun to amend its ways, that is when Christ will come back — after humanity has embraced Christianity and taken its own steps to make a peaceable kingdom and a peaceable Earth.

SIGNS AND SYMBOLS OF THE SECOND COMING

"So not everybody actually believes that there has to be these horrendous events right before Christ returns. There is an interpretive tradition that says differently."

Like Gary Stearman in the previous chapter, Denzler made reference to John Nelson Darby, the 19th Century preacher who proclaimed the rebirth of Israel, and Hal Lindsey, whose seminal work, "The Late, Great Planet Earth," continues to be a huge influence on people who believe in Biblical prophecy.

"Most people alive today don't realize," Denzler explained, "that 500 years ago, 1000 years ago, 1500 years ago, that's not how people read Revelation. All the things that we look at the book and say, 'Oh, it's so obvious.' It hasn't been obvious to millions of people for thousands of years before us. So Revelation was always a mysterious book. It barely was included in the canon, when the early Christian church was trying to figure out what belongs. There were many, many writings in the early Christian community, purporting to be from one apostle or another, or from Jesus himself. There were numerous gospels written about Jesus, not just the ones that we have in the New Testament today.

"It was a process of time through which some of these writings were highly valued and widely circulated, and as the church began to be more institutionalized, these writings were accepted as authoritative, inspired by God.

"Other writings were not," she said. "Some writings were very disputed, and one of those was the Book of Revelation. There was a large faction of early church leaders who did not think that Revelation was inspired and did not think it belonged in the canon. So that's my take on Revelation and violence. We think of Revelation as being a book of the Bible, the Bible being inspired by God. We think of everybody throughout history having understood Revelation just like we think we understand it today. And 'tain't so."

AND WHAT DO THE ALIENS MAKE OF ALL THIS?

The conversation then turned to where UFOs and their alien occupants fit in the overall picture Denzler has been painting. Again, her response was intelligent, thoughtful and certainly different.

"I think there's something to the UFO phenomenon," she said, "something that goes beyond it just being a psycho-genic or socio-genic thing. It's not just caused by mass hysteria and it's not just because individual people want to be special or everybody's always misidentifying stuff. I think there's something there. Not in every case. Not all sightings, of course. Many of them are misidentifications and some are hoaxes. But there is that remnant, that core that does seem to have some genuine stuff behind it, some something.

SIGNS AND SYMBOLS OF THE SECOND COMING

"The assumption is that whatever it is, is intelligent," she continued. "And so I've played little 'thought games' with myself for a couple of years now, about if I was an intelligent, space-faring species, and I came upon a planet like this, with the kinds of activities that we engage in, the kinds of beliefs that we hold, all over the face of the Earth, the kinds of expectations that people in different belief systems have, for what the future should be like or will be like, how would I react to these people?"

Denzler's "thought game" moved to phase two.

"It's very possible," she said, "that an intelligent species could arrive on Earth and figure out that, in terms of just raw power and dominance, there's a constellation of nations that seem to have it kind of crystallized in them, and that these nations, many of them believe in a thing they call Christianity. And when you look at the teachings of the Christians and the different beliefs that the different groups have, you'd get some idea about the popularity of this whole Second Coming idea.

"And it's plausible to me that an intelligent, space-faring species would say, 'You know, we could precipitate a really unpleasant situation if we showed up there like this. Because with those expectations built into those people, through 150 or 200 years of Darby-ist thinking, how are they going to take our arrival? Are they going to think that we're the antichrist before the Christ? Are they going to think we're the Christ? How are they going to handle this?'

"So it could plausibly be," Denzler said, "one reason why they haven't landed on the White House lawn: because they don't want to play into our religious expectations."

Denzler also touched on another, more familiar scenario.

"I know it's one that's popular," she said. "That they are the forces that are identified in the Biblical tradition as demons and demonic, that they are deceiving many people who believe that they are benevolent space aliens, and they're just waiting for the right time to strike, the right time to reveal themselves, when they think they can do so to maximum effect. And when they do that, then they will undermine the Christian faith and it will be in response to that that ultimately Christ is going to have to return, because it will be the only way the world can be saved. I know there's also a strain of that kind of thinking out there."

CONTACT WITH THE "INTERMEDIATE RACE"

Denzler offered still another fascinating possible scenario.

"It's occurred to me," she said, "that there is a race of intelligent entities

SIGNS AND SYMBOLS OF THE SECOND COMING

whose proper and natural home is in and around this Planet Earth. That we are not the highest evolutionary creatures in our tiny little corner of the universe here. That there are evolutionarily advanced intelligent species that in some senses are quote, unquote, 'higher than us.' What would happen if a space-faring race came and what they found was — there are so many ways that this could be split. Supposing that these other races are not physical in the way that we are, but they're not 'god-stuff' either? Of course, as you know, there's a long tradition of there being kind of an intermediate race of beings, somewhere between the divine realm and the physical human realm. People have posited this intermediate race of beings for a long, long time.

"Perhaps these beings' welfare," Denzler said, "is linked to our own. Kind of like our own welfare, whether we are fully conscious of it or not, is linked to the welfare of the cardinals hopping around out here on my patio now, or the dolphins and the whales. Our existence on this planet is tied to theirs. Our existence on this planet is tied to the existence of the trees. We are part of the system.

"There's no other species on Earth that has acquired the ability to manipulate our environment and to change the biosphere in wholesale, massive ways. Well, perhaps this intermediate species I was speaking of is also tied into this whole system, and so what happens, what we do, may be posing some kind of threat to the continued existence of this intermediate species. UFO sightings and abduction experiences could be a function of that."

And yet another scenario. What if we weren't part of the real alien contact event at all?

"What would happen," Denzler said, "if a space-faring race from elsewhere in the universe, either a para-physical or a thoroughly physical race, were to travel and to find our little corner of the universe? And what if the intelligent life forms it made contact with were the para-physical, intermediate race of beings that were around on this planet? What if the human race was looked at as a kind of a secondary, quasi-intelligent species kind of infesting the Earth? So what if the space-faring aliens have made contact with intelligent life on this planet, but the intelligent life they made contact with was not the human race? It was the intermediate race, that race of intelligent beings somewhere between the spiritual realm and the physical human realm. There are just so many different scenarios."

GUARDING AGAINST FALSE PROPHETS

After that fascinating glimpse into Denzler's sort of playful alien contact scenarios, a question regarding false prophets, like Charles Manson and Marshall Applewhite of Heaven's Gate, was asked.

SIGNS AND SYMBOLS OF THE SECOND COMING

"There have always been people like this," she replied. "Scholars of religion have gone back and looked at varieties of popular religious movements in the Middle Ages, popular religious movements in the time of Christ. Christ was by no means the only individual who appeared in Palestine in that timeframe claiming to be the Messiah. There were always messiahs popping their heads up, and Jesus of Nazareth was just another one of them, from the point of view of the Romans, and from the point of view of the Jews. There have always been people who would do that."

Denzler mentioned a book written by Charles Kimball called "When Religion Becomes Evil." According to Kimball, Denzler said, there are five warning signs for when a religion becomes corrupt and false.

"The first is absolute truth claims," Denzler said, "when you get somebody who claims to have the absolute truth. They have the knowledge, they have all the answers, and for a price, and it may not be a monetary price, it may be another kind of price, but for a price they'll share it with you. Because they have the absolute truth that nobody else has.

"Blind obedience," Denzler continued. "You need to have faith. Don't use reasoning. Don't use evidence. Don't think comparatively about this versus that. Here's the Word. Let me show you the Word. Let me show you the Way. Believe in me. They want blind obedience from you.

"Another sign is establishing the ideal time," she went on. "The time when it's all going to be better. It's going to be right over here. We're going to go to Jonestown and we're going to build the ideal community in the forest of Guyana. It will be a return to Utopia. It will be a just society with no more racism, no more hunger, no more poverty, no more want. The ideal time is now. You get the early Mormon settlers in Utah building the ideal community. You read a history of the Mormon community, and it's a little bit less than ideal because you have people in absolute, total control. They made absolute truth claims and they expected blind obedience from all of their followers.

"Number four," she said. "The End Justifies Any Means. Even if what we're doing might normally be considered kind of underhanded or sneaky or devious or illegal, when you're doing it for God, it's different. We're doing it for a good end. It's a good cause. Kind of like in the Children of God cult, led by David Moses Berg. They decided that one way to win people to Christ was through 'flirty fishing.' Basically, they expected female members of the group to prostitute themselves to try to get people to join, especially to get the support of the more wealthy businessmen around the globe. So any means that was possible, it was okay."

For number five on the false prophet list, "Declaring Holy War," Denzler

SIGNS AND SYMBOLS OF THE SECOND COMING

read aloud from Kimball's book.

"We have said that more wars have been waged, more people killed, and more evil perpetrated in the name of religion than by any other institutional force in human history. The sad truth continues in our present day. In somewhat different ways, leaders and combatants continue to depict their war as a holy cause. Declaring war 'holy' is a sure sign of corrupt religion. In fact, at the center of authentic religion, one always finds the promise of peace. Both an inner peace for the adherent and a requirement to seek peaceful coexistence with the rest of Creation. Perilous situations at times may indeed warrant the decisive use of force or forced military action, but such action must not be cloaked in religious language or justified by religion."

PUTTING OUR HOPES INTO TOMORROW

Denzler again returned to her experiences as a young woman in the fundamentalist cult.

"I lived for fifteen years," she recalled, "expecting the imminent return of Christ — like tomorrow. The church that I belonged to told me when it was going to happen, and they didn't just pick a day out of the hat. They claimed to have studied the Bible and studied the timetables of history and to really have worked hard on figuring out how to read the signs of the times and to read the seasons. They tried to explain it to all of us, and of course the way they did it, it sounded very reasonable. But then again, I had nothing to compare it with. I had no access to other information with which I could compare it, and they didn't tell me what the other information was, because that wasn't their job. They weren't about promoting the other guy's interpretation, too, and saying, 'Here are the varied interpretations. We think ours is best, but here are the others, just in case you agree with them.'

"And what they said seemed to make sense to me," she continued. "As much as I knew, it seemed to make sense. But it turned out not to be a winning approach to my daily life. It turned out not to be a winning approach to figuring out how to make our society as fair and just and peaceable as possible for today. Instead, we put all our hopes into tomorrow, into when Christ returned. That's where all our hopes were.

"People would go without medical care. People would go without dental care, 'Because really, when Christ comes back, he'll heal my rotten teeth, and then I won't have to go to the dentist. I won't have all the expense of going to the dentist.' I mean, people really did this. People would not prepare and plan to grow old and to need to retire, because Christ was going to return before they got old. So why bother saving for retirement? That turned out not to be a winning

SIGNS AND SYMBOLS OF THE SECOND COMING

strategy."

Even in that kind of spiritual darkness, however, there was an upside.

"The only thing that was good about it," Denzler said, "was that insofar as people wanted to be good people, to learn to behave properly, to follow the will of God, it gave you not just some kind of pie-in-the-sky, gee, when I die, maybe I'll go to heaven kind of thing, but this assurance that I'm going to get my reward for being good right now, while I'm still alive, in this physical body. And that made many of us be good and strive to do good.

"But like Saint Paul says, 'When I was a child, I thought as a child. But when I grew up, I put away childish things.' And I think that is where the problem with the hope in the literal return of Jesus Christ tomorrow lies, because it traps people in a stage of faith development that can keep them at a fairly unsophisticated level of spiritual maturity instead of allowing them to grow."

SIGNS AND SYMBOLS OF THE SECOND COMING

CHAPTER FIVE

THE COMING OF A NEW TEACHER

Were teachers like Christ and Buddha really extraterrestrials who came to Earth to raise the consciousness of mankind at great sacrifice to themselves? Are we also aliens of a kind, having lived many lifetimes on other worlds besides Earth?

While many believe the aliens are angelic or demonic, what if they are more accurately morally neutral in their regard for mankind? Does their involvement with the ancient peoples of this world continue to this day because of some form of crucial karmic necessity?

Why do some people long for the kind of leadership that takes choice away from them? How do false prophets obtain the blind obedience they always seem to demand? Do we secretly long to escape from freedom?

These are the kind of questions researcher and author G.C. Schellhorn raises in this chapter. Schellhorn's interest in UFOs began, as is so often the case, in childhood. At the age of twelve, while at a YMCA camp in the Missouri Ozarks, he sighted four UFOs.

"They came in over the low mountains," Schellhorn said, "and they were probably about a thousand or two yards above the mountains. They were very bright, very orange. They came in staggered formation about twenty seconds apart. So they weren't meteorites or comets or anything like that.

"Well, that worked on my mind," he continued, "over the years, off and on. It was 1952. That was the same year that there was a big flyover of UFOs in Wash-

SIGNS AND SYMBOLS OF THE SECOND COMING

ington, D.C. There was a lot of activity in the Missouri Ozarks then, too."

From that point in his youth, Schellhorn began to read UFO-related literature and stumbled across a book by NASA engineer Josef Blumrich called "The Spaceships of Ezekiel."

"When Blumrich went to the Book of Ezekiel," Schellhorn said, "and saw the description of the ship of the Lord as it landed, that's supposed to be God descending. When he read the description of the vessel, he recognized some of the things he'd been working on for NASA, like the kind of landing gear that's described there. He thought that for a non-technical people, the description was very accurate of the kind of landing gear he'd been working on."

Schellhorn decided to do his own independent research on the Bible and its relationship to the UFO phenomenon, which resulted in his book, "Extraterrestrials In Biblical Prophecy," first published in 1990 by Horus House Press.

"I didn't get it all there," Schellhorn said, "but I think I got 95 percent."

Schellhorn was born into a Presbyterian household but left the church at age twelve after coming to the conclusion that it was very corrupt and offered him little in the way of spiritual satisfaction.

"I kind of officially dropped out," he said. "Now, I believe in God. I don't know if you think you've got a down-to-earth, conventional Christian here, because you don't. But I definitely believe there is a Creator and we're all his sons and daughters. I'd classify myself as an independent and a freethinker beyond that."

THE NATURE OF PROPHECY

Before discussing the Second Coming directly, Schellhorn took a few moments to provide some background on prophecy in general.

"There are things about prophecy," he said, "that I don't think many people consider. If you go back even as far as the Bronze Age times, or before that, we've got evidence of prognostications and soothsaying of various kinds. But when you talk about prophecy in the Western World, you're usually referring to Judaism, Christianity and Islam. Prophecy in the Judeo-Christian sense is a foretelling of things to come with a divine inspiration added to it. Whereas soothsaying, fortune telling and prognostications of other kinds very often don't have any divine inspiration involved with them.

"We've had several major prophets," he continued, "and we usually ascribe to them divine intervention. They think, whether they were accurate or not, that they are speaking to the Lord. Judaism in general believes that Yahweh is God

SIGNS AND SYMBOLS OF THE SECOND COMING

himself speaking to them. But if we study the ancient Sumerian, Babylonian and Akkadian texts, I think there is a lot of evidence that Yahweh is a tribal god and that he is a commander of those extraterrestrials that were also visiting Sumer and Babylon and Akkadia at that time.

"And it appears," Schellhorn said, "that these extraterrestrials divided up the territory and had a great deal of influence and were actually guiding the politics of these various nations. So that definitely ties UFOs and extraterrestrials with the early books of the Bible, and greatly influences the thinking that later pervaded Judaism and Christianity."

THE SEDUCTIVE LURE OF BEING A PROPHET

Following the discussion of prophecy as inspired by God, Schellhorn next addressed the thorny issue of false prophets.

"It's seductive to want to be a prophet," Schellhorn said. "There's a lot of power involved in it, too, if you're successful at all. We have quite a few people that are claiming that they're prophets of one kind or another. Many of them are claiming that they're getting their material directly from God, and it's caused some real confusion. Jim Jones is a good case of that. David Koresh and the tragic happenings in Waco are a good example of that.

"I think there have always been a lot of false prophets in the world," he continued. "When we talk about the End Times, it's a problematic question, because I can say myself that the world is someday going to come to an end. I can say that there are going to be massive earth changes in the future. I can say that there's a large probability that we're going to have an axis shift. I can say, 'Sometime soon.'

"And what does that mean? What does 'soon' mean? I can say that there will be evil or negative people that try to control the destiny of this planet and cause confusion and wars and tribulations of various kinds. I'm quite sure those things will happen, but I'm not going to call myself a prophet just because I think those are probabilities."

One complicating factor, according to Schellhorn, is the nature of time itself.

"There's a problem with time and the timeline in prophecies," he said. "I've read a lot of material about contactees and what they've been told by their extraterrestrial contactors. Many of them have been told, 'Well, such and such will happen pretty soon.' What does 'pretty soon' mean? I'm not so sure that extraterrestrial time is on the same continuum as Earth time is, because what might be a short time to an extraterrestrial might be quite some time in Earth terms.

SIGNS AND SYMBOLS OF THE SECOND COMING

"If what quantum physics seems to be telling us is true," Schellhorn continued, "maybe the past, present and future are, in some way that we find hard to imagine, all occurring at the same moment. Therefore it is possible to look into the future and see what might happen, although the attempts to do that in the past seem to me to be suspect. We don't have any real evidence that any of those attempts have been very successful.

"I remember Billy Meier, the Swiss contactee. He said that he was taken forward in time in a craft and visited the Earth a couple of hundred years from now. He was also taken backward in time and saw dinosaurs on the planet's surface. I don't know how much credibility we can give those statements, although I am impressed with the early contacts that Billy Meier has had and what he says happened. I'm also impressed with the early photographs, which so many people tried to debunk. I know the Japanese did a pretty thorough job on those photographs, and they came to the conclusion that they were legitimate."

When considering Meier's claims, as Schellhorn demonstrates, one can only wonder whether it is possible to travel in time or to perceive past, present and future as just three aspects of an "Eternal Now."

WILL JESUS HIMSELF RETURN?

Meanwhile, Schellhorn's view of the Second Coming departs from the usual Biblical understanding.

"I know that many religions," he said, "have prophesied a Second Coming. The Hebrews believe the first one hasn't happened yet, so they're still waiting. When we consider Hinduism, some of their ancient texts say that there will be twenty-four incarnations of Krishna, which is the incarnated Vishnu. They put the last incarnation as number eight, so that would suggest that there are many more incarnations of Krishna to come.

"In my mind," Schellhorn continued, "I wonder if Jesus as we know him in the New Testament will come or whether there won't be another great teacher. Just like the Buddhists expected another great teacher, the Maitreya Buddha to appear. When we talk about Christ and Christ Consciousness, we move a little bit beyond the man Jesus himself

"I believe that the great prophets of the past, such as Buddha, Mohamed and Jesus, are advanced spiritual entities that have probably had Earth lives in the past but have also had lives in many dimensions. They're more advanced mentally and spiritually than the entities on this planet and so they come back with the idea of teaching."

We're all here to learn, Schellhorn explained, and that learning determines

SIGNS AND SYMBOLS OF THE SECOND COMING

how we progress through our various reincarnations.

"I see these great teachers," he said, "Christ, Buddha, Mohamed, and others, as entities that have come back. They're familiar with life on Planet Earth, as such. They come back and offer their services and they usually raise the consciousness of the people on the planet's surface at that time to one degree or another."

Schellhorn next posed a very interesting question.

"Now, is it necessary," he asked, "that the entity that we call Jesus, that he himself return? I know many Christians would insist on that, that it has to be the same entity. I'm not so convinced that it does have to be the same entity. I am convinced that there will be other great teachers in the future, that appear and offer their services, but I'm not convinced that it has to be the same entity that we see in the New Testament. It could be another entity, another like entity, one that was at the same level of mental and spiritual development as he was.

"After all," he said, "if you want to be practical, what would be the difference? As long as the messages are approximately akin, does it have to be the same actual entity? It might be. I don't know. I don't think any of us do."

Still, the hope in the return of the New Testament Jesus continues to be a cherished one by many of the faithful.

"I think it's in human nature," Schellhorn said. "Our spiritual self, realizing the shortcomings of this world and of our own development, yearns for that sort of thing. There is a mass desire on the part of people on the globe in general, and a more specified desire among various religious groups, that someone come and help them 'elevate,' uplift themselves mentally and especially spiritually. It's the spiritual spark that's inside of everyone that yearns for a new teacher to pull them upward."

THE ANTICHRIST IN REVELATION

Schellhorn believes that there is no one single antichrist prophesied in Revelation.

"When John wrote about the antichrist," Schellhorn said, "it was plural. Most people don't realize that. When you go back to the earliest translations, you'll see that it isn't singular in the text. I don't have a problem in my own mind in seeing a lot of antichrists. We've got at any time in the world quite a few antichrists that are operative. We could say Saddam Hussein, Idi Amin, Hitler. There are an innumerable number of people who seem to qualify at any given moment. Some a little bit more abominable than others, but they're there. Christianity has insisted on in-

SIGNS AND SYMBOLS OF THE SECOND COMING

terpreting the scriptures as having one antichrist. That's another example of how widely divergent different interpretations can be."

Schellhorn cautions that we should take into account when the Book of Revelation was written and says he does not believe that every prophecy given in the mysterious book will come true.

"I see it more as a symbolic text," he said, "written by a very mystical man of whom we know very, very little. There is so much there that it is easy to take a piece of it and say, 'Well, this is happening right now,' or for that matter has happened in the past. But as far as pointing to one person in the world that is extant at this moment or is to come and say that he's the antichrist, I can't do that, personally. I think we'd be much better off to sort out the really negative influences and individuals that we've got operating on the planet today and do more to keep them on a tight leash rather than worrying about fulfilling everything that the Book of Revelation speaks of."

DREAMS OF THE NEW AGE

From the negativity associated with the various antichrists, the conversation shifted to something more hopeful.

"If this world manages to survive long enough," Schellhorn said, "there will be a New Age. If people gradually rise in their mental and spiritual being, if they learn, in other words, then you will have a New Age of peace and love. But it isn't in the immediate offing. I'm convinced of that. It's a very gradual thing.

"I believe humans come back," he continued, "and return again and again until they master mental and some spiritual control of themselves. The ones who do go on to other planes of existence. Maybe they don't come back to Earth, because in my estimation and the estimation of many philosophers and prophets of the past, the level of spirituality on this planet isn't very high."

Still, Earth is what Schellhorn called a "melting pot."

"Not only is it a melting pot," he said, "there are probably not many inhabited worlds that have the 'polychrome,' the various races, that this one does. I think most of them are probably 'monochrome,' just one race of one color, let's say, and one language. We're a real melting pot here, maybe a kind of an experiment. We're a 'growing ground.'

"I believe there are worlds far less developed than this one,'" he continued, "and when entities reach a certain point and they're ready for this world, they're likely to enter it."

Schellhorn said that progressing to the higher realms of existence takes place

SIGNS AND SYMBOLS OF THE SECOND COMING

ore on an individual level as opposed to the mass experience something like the Second Coming would entail. Individuals who have attained a certain mental and spiritual level, by experience and their lives on Earth, are "taken" to a new and higher plane of existence.

"When I say 'higher realms,'" he said, "we don't hear or read much about them in the Christian New Testament. But in the Hebrew holy texts, they do have definite ideas about different planes of existence, about the seven heavens and that sort of thing. There is a progression as the person grows from one level to a higher level. So it's not totally alien to the Judeo-Christian way of thinking."

THE ISSUE OF LEADERSHIP

Along the path to individual attainment of the New Age there are also many thorny obstacles to add to the difficulty of the journey.

"In this day and age," Schellhorn said, "and I suppose in past history as well, people are hungry for mental and spiritual knowledge. Some more than others, but they are. And they're hungry for direction. The problem is that many politicians and false prophets — like the Jim Joneses and the David Koreshes and the Charles Mansons, what have you — encourage them to follow and listen and to abide by what the prophet says. And they like to be told or they submit to being told how to live, what to think and what to do.

"I don't believe," he continued, "from the philosophers of history and the religious thinkers that have impressed me most in my life, that that's the way it works. Some of the eastern gurus will say, 'All I can do is point the way to you. I can't live it for you. You have to discover who you are and where you're going.' But too many people are, in a sense, mentally and spiritually lazy."

Schellhorn moved on to talk about a book written by famed psychoanalyst Erich Fromm called "Escape From Freedom."

"I think every American ought to read that today," Schellhorn said. "Because what he says is that the human tendency, generally speaking, is to let governments and leaders of various kinds make up the rules of living and then one follows those rules. In other words, one doesn't have to think about it; one doesn't have to exercise their mind.

"But what is all-important is that these governments or religions or what have you create the illusion of freedom, so that the individual thinks he's free. He likes the idea. He would not want to be told that he's not free, but in fact he likes other people doing the distasteful work that maintaining freedom would call for.

"They want these leaders, very often these 'prophets' that they choose, to

SIGNS AND SYMBOLS OF THE SECOND COMING

give them direction. In my experience, and from what I've' learned, if you're going to make large steps in growth, mentally and spiritually, you have to learn to do that within yourself. Nobody's going to make you mentally more acute or understanding. Nobody's going to make you more spiritually active and loving other than yourself. But people join groups and political parties and religions because they believe this will be bestowed on them.

"And I don't believe," he went on, "that that is really the way it is. There's a problem in many religions, too, with the smugness that goes along with it. Many Christians believe that if you're not a Christian, for instance, you're not a saved soul as such, or you're not going to heaven. But this rules out 75 percent of the total population of this planet. Still, many Christians believe that. I'm sure many Muslims believe that if you don't have faith that Mohamed is the last prophet of God that you're not going to heaven as well."

Schellhorn said he believes instead that we are all sons and daughters of God.

"I mean literally," he said, "we're all sons and daughters of God. Christians have trouble with that, generally speaking. But in the Gospels and elsewhere in the New Testament, very often, when a Christian runs across the phrase 'Son of God,' he thinks that that's Jesus, and Jesus is the Son of God and they're somewhat lesser. I would say lesser only to the extent that they're not the developed spiritual being that this great teacher was."

Schellhorn offered the Parable of the Mustard Seed to further bolster his argument.

"Christ talks about the mustard seed," he said, "and moving mountains. He says that if you have faith the size of a mustard seed you too could move mountains and do even greater things than he did. I don't think Christians know what to do with that. It seems to me that Jesus was saying that you could reach the same mental and spiritual level that he was at and even go beyond him.

"To me, those lines, those verses, open up a great hope, a prompting that people can develop. And here's the thing: God forbid, we might even become as wise, as loving, as peaceful and as spiritual as Jesus was. Maybe even become Christs on another planet for another wave of living entities somewhere else in the cosmos, just like he did. But the churches and the standard doctrine shy away from those considerations."

THE NATURE OF THE ALIENS

The aliens are not here, according to Schellhorn, to usher in the Second Coming. He said he basically agrees with a Brazilian Ufologist named A.J. Gevaerd,

SIGNS AND SYMBOLS OF THE SECOND COMING

to concluded that most of the UFO entities that are visiting Planet Earth seem to be neutral in their attitude toward humanity.

"I think they're here observing and studying," Schellhorn said. "After all, we're a polychrome, polyglot world probably very much unlike the other worlds out there. We have tremendous problems. We're at crucial moments in our development, with threats of nuclear weapons and war hanging over our heads. So we're a good sociological study, if you like. Gevaerd said he thought that the great majority of the extraterrestrials were neutral, a few were friendly, and a very few were hostile. From all my studies and experience, I tend to agree with that statement.

"Now the few that are friendly," Schellhorn continued, "I suspect that some of them are friendly because they're intimately involved with the history of this planet. As far back as Sumerian and Babylonian times, into Egyptian/Hebrew times, and right up to the present. Their 'karma,' if you like, to use a Buddhist expression, is involved with this planet and with us. They have influenced the course of events on this planet, and therefore their karma is involved. That might explain part of the interest.

"I believe that our teachers," he went on, "come from other worlds. Our prophets, our real, legitimate prophets, our great teachers, may have had many Earth lives. I think that probably Jesus had quite a few Earth lives. It appears that Buddha did. It makes sense. If you are going to come to a world as a teacher, it would be advisable to be very familiar with that world.

"So it's quite possible that some of these teachers such as Jesus are extraterrestrials in that sense. Anyone coming from another world to this world is an extraterrestrial. By the way, that makes many of us extraterrestrials because many of us have had a part or much of our growth in other worlds before we have had our Earth lives. I define extraterrestrial as an entity, a spiritual being, that has incarnated but who has had a majority of their development in another world, even though they may be living at this moment on Planet Earth. Whereas a true Earthling would be someone who has had the majority of their experience, mental and spiritual, and lived most of their lives on this planet.

"So I think these teachers are coming or have come from other worlds, other planes of existence that are higher mentally and spiritually. They've come here to do service. We should be very grateful that they're willing to do that, because life on this planet for most prophets, for most real prophets, isn't very comfortable. It can lead to crucifixion and other rather blatant, hostile reactions."

SIGNS AND SYMBOLS OF THE SECOND COMING

WHAT WE DON'T KNOW

But there is still so much that remains unknown, Schellhorn said.

"One thing I have learned," he said, "is that we know so very little. It bothers me sometimes to see that our scientists and our Ufologists as well as many people in religion believe that they know so much — that we as humans know so much and they personally know so much. I don't believe our science is very far progressed. As has happened in the past in medicine and physics and all of the sciences, people will be looking back in 200 years and saying, 'Oh, my God, they believed that? They were really primitive. They knew so little.' That seems to be the way history progresses.

"Although my ideas have changed from one decade to another," he continued, "and some of them drastically, I'm convinced that, even though there is so much that we don't know, we're learning more every day. And that's why we're here. We're here to learn. As long as human beings keep their hearts and minds open, I think they continue to progress, and happily so."

Schellhorn hearkened back to the earlier discussion of contactee Billy Meier.

"They were supposedly Pleiadeians that he was in contact with," Schellhorn said, "and he asked them once about their religion. They said, 'Well, we don't really have a religion, but everyone believes what they want to believe and no one holds that against them. They're totally entitled to their own beliefs. We're not sure about exactly what God is.' But they suggested that they didn't deny that there was a God, they just didn't know exactly what God is. We don't either.

"But then they said, 'One thing we find that keeps us going is that as we keep exploring the cosmos, we keep learning so much more. It drives us on and on. It's fascinating.' I kind of put myself in that position mentally. I'm very curious about the future of this planet and about what's out there in space.

"I'm also very curious about my God," Schellhorn said. "There's a lot I don't know, but I like to think I'm definitely willing to learn."

SIGNS AND SYMBOLS OF THE SECOND COMING

CHAPTER SIX

A RETURN TO SPIRITUALITY

Are the current anxieties some experience about an all-out Second Coming and Armageddon in the skies based simply on collective nightmarish memories of the past? Do we all unconsciously dread a recurrence of the terrifying warfare between different races of aliens as they fought in ancient times for dominance on Planet Earth?

Why were the leaders of the Heaven's Gate cult so sure that they and their followers would all experience the joy of a literal physical resurrection by means of a UFO? Could nothing have swayed them in their determination to use such a tragic delusion as the basis for their suicides?

Is the Book of Revelation truly a necessary component of the Bible? Do the ways we interpret it today create unfounded fears in an already jittery population, still reeling from terrorist attacks and the misery of ongoing warfare?

Brad Steiger is the author of over 150 books on every aspect of the paranormal, including "Revelation: The Divine Fire," "Gods of Aquarius," "UFOs and the Transformation of Man," "Mysteries of Time and Space," and more recently, "Real Ghosts, Restless Spirits and Haunted Places." He also coauthored, along with his wife Sherry, "The Encyclopedia of the Unknown and Unexplained," a three-volume set.

With that kind of absorption in supernatural mysteries, Steiger said that people are often surprised to hear that he comes from an evangelical Christian background.

"So you're kind of born with a Bible in your hand," Steiger said. "In confir-

SIGNS AND SYMBOLS OF THE SECOND COMING

mation class, we were given many Bible verses a week to memorize. In school, we had a religion class every day until junior high school, and, of course, we went to church on the weekend. Then I went to parochial college. I guess I was just born into the Bible. I've always found it to be a source of strength and inspiration."

Back in the late 1950s, Steiger discovered the field of UFO research.

"My first field of interest," he said, "was psychical research, and I saw the UFO phenomenon as being an extension of psychical research. I thought that contactees were our modem day mediums, and that the message they were saying was essentially the same thing that spiritualists and prophets had been saying. I'm not denying the extraterrestrial possibility, but I still think the UFO phenomenon is largely a paranormal, psychic phenomenon or a spiritual phenomenon. I think it's an extension of what we basically are as human beings."

CHANGING PERCEPTIONS OF THE SECOND COMING

Steiger said his feelings regarding the Second Coming have changed considerably from when he was a youth in Bible class.

"I now feel that Jesus of Nazareth," he said, "was born at a time when there were many apocalyptic sects in the Jewish faith. There was a strong belief that the Messiah would be coming soon. They were under oppression from the Romans and there certainly was a great impetus to hope that a Messiah was coming soon."

When he was asked to deal with the verses from Matthew Sixteen in which Jesus promises that some of those with him would not taste death, Steiger replied, "In my reading, I believe that Jesus taught us about the Way. He said that the Kingdom of Heaven is within. I believe that when he said we would not taste death, he meant that because we are spiritual beings, we do not taste eternal death. There is the death of the physical body, but the spirit lives on. So those standing before him, or those who hear his words today, if they believe and accept that they are spiritual beings, and maybe even if they don't, there is no death. There is only a change of worlds."

Although it can be argued that the Kingdom of Heaven is indeed within, a great many people still look forward to a literal, physical Second Coming.

"We have almost a template," he explained, "in our psyche. We want to be delivered. We want to find deliverance. Just to give some perspective to what I'm saying now — perhaps the reason that the Jews don't accept Jesus as the Messiah is because when the Messiah comes, the world changes. There is the judgment, then there is peace and love and everything's right with the world. And obviously, after Jesus died, there isn't love and peace and everything isn't right with the world. So that's why they're still waiting."

SIGNS AND SYMBOLS OF THE SECOND COMING

THE NEVER-ENDING END TIMES

Steiger said that throughout history there has long been the expectation that the End Times were at hand.

"Certainly in the 12th Century," he said, "they thought they were the End Times, and the 15th Century was the End Times. When they had the crossbow it had to be the End Times, and then the same when they developed gun powder. Those were all bringing the End Times. And after the atom bomb came, okay, now we know it has to be the End Times. But we're still kind of struggling. Maybe Judgment Day, Jesus is telling us, is really every day. We should live always as if we are going to be called to account for our misdeeds. Maybe we're living always on the precipice of going to Eternal Life, so we should live as if every day was Judgment Day."

Even Christopher Columbus had an End Times mentality, according to Steiger.

"Columbus was a great believer," Steiger said, "in apocalyptic literature. He was an apocalyptic. So he believed that when he found this new land, that now Jesus would come for certain. There was plenty of room for the believers and the millennium would surely come. We have been apocalyptic in the United States ever since our nation began. We have the preachers that are a familiar part of the frontier.

"America to some," he continued, "is the new Atlantis. To some it is the Promised Land. We are kind of geared to the idea that the United States will bring about this new era, this new Golden Age.

"And then we have the religionists who will tie it in with the return of Christ. Now the hope for the return of Jesus, for the believer in establishment Christianity or fundamentalist Christianity, is strong, because there is a fervent wish that Jesus will come and deliver us from this terrible mess we're in. That is basically the human condition. We have always looked to the hills, we have always looked to the skies, for a deliverer. Well, then, what do we have? We have the UFO! We have the signs in the skies. We have the wonders in the sky. Wow!"

IS REVELATION REALLY HELPFUL?

Steiger was asked about his beliefs regarding the Book of Revelation. As before, his feelings were much changed from his childhood days in Bible class.

"To me, the Book of Revelation," he said, "should never have been included in the Bible. Whoever wrote the Book of Revelation — now, of course, we thought at first it was the Apostle John. Now we simply say 'John the Revelator,' because

SIGNS AND SYMBOLS OF THE SECOND COMING

we really don't know. It was probably written by a prophet or visionary on the Greek Island of Patmos. Some have said that maybe he was high on drugs and maybe he was chewing some herbs that made him see things.

"I don't think we need to go there," he continued, "but I think we should say that this was a man who was passionate about the persecution the Christians were undergoing at the time. He saw a time when Nero was really going to get his. Using the Hebrew alphabet, we find that the numerical value for 'Nero Caesar' is 666."

The reference in Revelation to the "seven-headed beast" also corresponds to the seven hills on which Rome is built, Steiger explained.

"Rome was the dominant ruler," Steiger said. "The Emperor ruled the entire known world at that time, and the Christians were being persecuted. So what he's really saying, in symbolic, allegorical terms, is 'Be of faith. Be of strong faith, because Rome isn't going to last forever. Rome is going to fall. Nero isn't going to be in power forever, the angels have come to tell me. There are good times ahead.'

"Now, again, the Book of Revelation was nearly omitted from the Bible. I think there are many, many works of faith that should have been included in our Bible, and I'm of the opinion that the Book of Revelation is not one of those."

THE WORDS OF THE SPACE BROTHERS

But even without lending credence to the doom-saying of the Book of Revelation, as Steiger prefers not to do, there are still valid warnings of the dangerous times the human race is enduring.

"There are definite signs," he said, "that seem to indicate to us that something we're doing as a species is very wrong. We're going to have to get straight about things. We go back to the earliest of prophets and then we go back to the most contemporary of the UFO contactees. We say that there are these entities, whether they're Space Brothers or whether they're angels, and, of course, we could argue that they might be one and the same, who are basically saying the same things. Humans must love one another, they must love this planet, they must be open to a spiritual change, and they must be open to a transformation from homo sapiens to 'homo spiritus.' They must begin to move on from emphasizing things of physicality, the 'physical-ness' of life. They must be more aware, perceptive of the spiritual aspects of life. So the message stays the same."

But this continually offered message seems to get by us all somehow.

"I think that it's obvious,'" Steiger said, "that we never 'get it,' as a species. Each century we start over again, to a large degree. As with the myths of Atlantis,

SIGNS AND SYMBOLS OF THE SECOND COMING

which say that there was a great Golden Age and then there were some people around to muck it up. It was destroyed, and we start over. That seems to be the seasonal, cyclical template that's in our collective psyche. There is no end and no beginning, and somehow this concept of the world ending, or Judgment Day coming, gives us another chance.

"When Jesus comes," he continued, "there's a thousand years where all the good guys get to reign. The devil gets thrown down into the pit. All of these good things are happening. What do the Space Brothers say? Well, if we really get it together, we're going to translate into this higher dimension of being and reality. It's kind of the same message, though each new version gets doctored a bit.

"The message part doesn't change, but the interpreter does, because our culture changes. It becomes more technological, so some of the language changes to convey this message. But basically it's been the same message throughout all of our spiritual evolution, which is that we are more than physical beings. And the Second Coming, this great time of revelation, is going to be when our species makes that quantum leap into that new being that we are evolving toward.

"This is our odyssey," he said. "This is our space odyssey. This is our Second Coming. This is our second birth. This is our reemergence as spiritual beings rather than physical beings."

IS IT ALL JUST A BAD MEMORY?

But what about the UFO phenomenon and its relationship to the Second Coming? Do the Space Brothers, for example, indicate that a cosmic "Star Wars" with Jesus in the lead role might be on the horizon?

"I think these kinds of things," Steiger replied, "are 'memories' that we have. We have this memory of this great warfare, which occurred in our quote, unquote, 'beginning.' I don't think it's what's coming. It's what's been. In the Mahabharata and the Baghavad Gita, in the sacred works of India, we find the vimanas, the spaceships.

"The vimanas operate by thought," he went on, "and have this great ray that destroys elephants and cities and every opposition that rises to confront them. We have the evidence of Sodom and Gomorrah. We have evidence of these ancient cities that were burnt. We know that in siege they would burn one another's cities. But in these cities of stone there was such heat that they would become crystalline. They merged to green glass in some instances, which appeared to be evidence of nuclear bombs or some kind of incredible energy and power.

"So I think that they're memories of when we were probably crouching behind boulders and watching these beings duke it out in the air and on the ground.

SIGNS AND SYMBOLS OF THE SECOND COMING

Then we kind of arise from the ashes. What we have memories of and then project as the Second Corning is really this warfare that we saw in ancient times between extraterrestrials or some kind of multi-dimensional beings. That's in our collective unconscious."

AND THE FEAR PERSISTS

"Why do we have this fear?" Steiger asked rhetorically. "Why do we have this apprehension?

"I think it's our fear that it's going to come around again," he said. "So each century, when there is some dramatic invention that can be used for ill as well as good, and generally is used for ill, is used for warfare, these fears arise. With the advent of nuclear power, we of course have UFOs. Even though UFOs have been with us as long as we've stood upright and before, and may be the reason we stood upright in the first place, we still announce the beginning of saucers in our contemporary time as being synonymous almost with the advent of nuclear power. That's when people seemed to be seeing these signs in the sky. The signs were immediately interpreted by the conventional religionists as signs of the Second Coming of Christ.

"I think we cannot deny that this nation is overwhelmingly Christian," he continued, "at least nominally Christian. Everyone's heard, if they paid attention in Sunday school at all, they've heard something about Revelation. They've heard something about the Second Coming. This is a time of deliverance, but I think people also have a fear because in the Second Coming, not everyone makes it. There is this big army. There is the big clash of good and evil."

Steiger next made reference to the movie "Return of the King" from the "Lord of the Rings" trilogy.

"To me," he said, "that is almost transparently allegorical to the Second Coming, where all the good beings gather to fight the forces of evil. And if they lose, this is it. We also have the fiery pit, don't we, in 'Lord of the Rings'? This is such an impression on the psyche. The Christian Church and its teachings have been essentially dominant in the Western World since probably at least the 4th Century. So we have many generations of visualizing this great last warfare, this Armageddon, this showdown between good and evil. Then, of course, in Islam they have the same kind of Armageddon situation, so that the great Abrahamic religions of the world do see a great final conflict between good and evil."

THE ANTICHRIST AS ALLEGORY

Just as Steiger sees the Battle of Armageddon as basically a race memory being projected into the future, he also does not believe in the coming of a literal

SIGNS AND SYMBOLS OF THE SECOND COMING

antichrist.

"Every pope since the Reformation," he said, "has been named the antichrist. Any powerful figure becomes the antichrist. But again, we have to look at the antichrist symbolically. What is he? He's someone who appears very good, who is doing good deeds and is healing, but then he's really serving Satan. I think the antichrist is allegorical to the struggle within each human being. We have the good and we have the bad and we must always be vigilant, we must always choose to do the right thing."

But what if the antichrist is real and even has UFOs in his arsenal?

"If truly these are extraterrestrial beings," Steiger said, "if they are reconnoitering our planet, if they do plan an invasion, we know within our heart of hearts that we don't have a chance against that kind of technology. It would be so much worse than the Conquistadors with gunpowder and steel coming up against the spears of the Inca or the Maya or the Aztec. The idea of meeting that type of superior culture, if they intended ill, is again that fear that we have that there is a powerful army that we would be unable to oppose. Which would then cause, as we see happening right now with the war on terror, this feeling of helplessness. We have this feeling of militancy because we have to guard against this invasion."

In response to that grim picture, Steiger sees a rebirth of spiritual instincts in the people as they struggle to cope with so much uncertainty.

"We're seeing a return to spirituality," he said. "We're seeing a return to serious study of the paranormal. We're seeing a return to people putting their seats in church pews. And we're also seeing a great belief in the Second Coming, a Second Coming that will deliver us from all this evil and potential evil. All of these things are working together right now for an intensification of belief in the Second Coming. Because Lordy me, we want deliverance."

HEAVEN'S GATE AND THE PHYSICAL RESURRECTION

Among the many books Steiger has written is one he co-authored with UFO researcher Hayden Hewes called "UFO Missionaries Extraordinary," about the Heaven's Gate cult, written nearly 20 years before the infamous mass suicide in San Diego in 1997. In the wake of the tragic suicides, the book was reissued as "Inside Heaven's Gate."

Steiger discussed, from his own firsthand perspective, the bizarre belief in an alien form of Second Coming that the members of Heaven's Gate were willing to die for. Steiger said that cult leaders "Bo" and "Peep"' truly believed what they were preaching.

SIGNS AND SYMBOLS OF THE SECOND COMING

"We sat there night after night," Steiger recounted, "and I tried every little trick in the book to say, 'Oh, come on now. Just between us.' But they believed. They believed that they had been given this role in the Second Coming. Now, they didn't see it in terms of the conventional Christian aspects, but they did see it as moving to a higher level, to the Father. And they saw it then as a physical resurrection.

"People mocked them for this belief," he continued, "but if we look at the strict Christian interpretation, it is a physical resurrection. Every believer rises physically from the dead. That's why, until recently, and I'm sure even still, cremation has never been popular because there goes your body. There is this belief that's been instilled, and it has been for centuries, that you need those bones. Just like in the valley where the Lord made all the bones have flesh again, you're going to need that body, because it's a physical resurrection.

"That's a strong belief in all the Abrahamic religions, that there is a physical resurrection. So Bo and Peep were not departing from orthodoxy that much in saying that. But then they combined it with the UFO phenomenon, saying that it would be UFOs as the vehicle that would transport those who believed, those who accepted. They would physically go to that next dimension."

Steiger said he would try to get Bo and Peep to hedge a little on that interpretation.

"I would say to them, 'You're rational people. Surely you mean in the spirit.' And they said, 'Oh, no, we are going physically.' And that's why, of course, the whole idea of the mass suicide. The bodies then would be taken. They would literally be resurrected on that next level in their physical bodies.

"Now, I'm not saying that this belief in a physical resurrection is a prevailing belief today, but it certainly was for centuries, that the body was not to be cremated. People who were cremated, or were burned at the stake, of course, were heretics. They didn't need their bodies because they were going to hell. But the true believer would have a place of rest for his mortal shell because he's going to need it again."

AN IDEA WHOSE TIME HAS COME

In spite of false prophets and other snares of disappointment on the path, the belief in an imminent Second Coming seems to be getting more popular all the time.

"There are people who believe they have seen the truth," Steiger said. "You've checked the websites, and they're proliferating, as people feel strongly that the Second Coming will happen soon. We had this series of books, you know, that promote the whole idea of being taken, being lifted up, with the physical

SIGNS AND SYMBOLS OF THE SECOND COMING

body. "The Left Behind" series. That had become an incredibly popular series. I can't believe that there could be a popular fiction series about the Rapture. Still, I know personally many people who take that literally and they're just waiting at any moment. There will just be a pile of clothes and they will be taken up.

"There again," he continued, "it's the idea of physical deliverance, isn't it? Because it isn't their body there in the pile of clothes. It's just the pile of clothes. So this idea of being physically taken to another plane is becoming increasingly popular. We're going to have an increasing number of people who have visions. You know, as in the Old Testament Book of Joel, 'Your old men shall see visions and your young men shall dream dreams.' We're going to have more and more of that as war becomes more prevalent, as the war on terror escalates, as there are going to be more bombings. We're going to have a desperate longing for a Second Coming to end all this mess and grant us all deliverance."

Steiger again allows that his own personal beliefs about the Second Coming are not of the orthodox kind described above.

"I think the Second Coming would occur," he said, "when everyone realizes and embraces what Jesus and all the other avatars are talking about. Recognizing, respecting one another. Loving one another as yourself. When you look into the eyes of your brother and your sister and you're seeing the eyes of God looking back at you and recognizing that oneness. Again, we're talking idealistically. We're talking about an Edenic paradise, which probably, I believe, will never happen.

"I believe this is Schoolhouse Earth," he continued. "I believe what Jesus is telling us is that we must accept our personal responsibility for our actions. We are evolving into higher beings, but maybe we don't make it the first time. Maybe we come back and repeat seventh grade over again. We have that opportunity. I think that Earth is a place of learning. Earth is a place where we make mistakes and where we make successes, where we can truly evolve as a species.

"An ideal world," Steiger said, "would be one where everyone accepts the oneness at the same time. But I think again, Schoolhouse Earth. Some people are in kindergarten, some people are in junior high, and some people are getting their Ph.D.s. So I'm not optimistic about it ever happening at the same time, but if it could happen, if there could be that type of dramatic burst, that quantum leap for the entire species at the same moment — that would be co-equivalent to the Second Coming."

SIGNS AND SYMBOLS OF THE SECOND COMING

CHAPTER SEVEN

LOST IN TRANSLATION

Is a tribe of Indians in Peru being readied for a kind of Second Coming as filtered through their own cultural expectations? Are the Star Gods they put their faith in giving them a message nearly identical to that imparted to Christians anticipating the return of Jesus?

Will ancient prophecies of the Mark of the Beast soon be a reality? Does the seemingly innocent Universal Product Code conceal the threat of future mass economic enslavement to the totalitarian government of the antichrist?

How can we guard ourselves and our loved ones from the evil snares of the world, which draw ever tighter as the days go by? Will we, as individuals, ever learn the kind of love and compassion needed for mankind's tenuous collective existence to continue?

Sherry Hansen Steiger, author/coauthor of 40 books, is the wife of the prolific author and researcher Brad Steiger, who was interviewed separately in the previous chapter. Like her husband, Sherry was born into a devoutly Bible-believing household.

SIGNS AND SYMBOLS OF THE SECOND COMING

"I was actually raised, until the age of about eight, by my grandparents," Sherry said, "who were from Sweden and were evangelicals in the church they went to. It was the Evangelical United Brethren, which has now been merged into a Methodist church. But they were very fundamental. My grandfather was caretaker of the church and it seemed like my life was in the church.

"But I always felt somehow," she continued, "deep in my heart, that I've landed on a different planet. I can even remember as far back as looking through the bars of my crib and wondering why people treat one another so poorly? The feeling that I had in my heart, that things should be different here on this planet — it seems that people should know that the teachings I was exposed to every day at church, to love one another, was really what we should be doing. Why is there quibbling? Why is there arguing?"

Sherry said that as she grew older, she found it harder to accept the standard answers that had been imparted to her.

"When I was old enough to start asking my own questions," she said, "the religious questions that I had didn't seem to fit with any particular denomination or any particular set of answers. My grandparents didn't particularly like my beliefs, nor did my parents. My inner feeling was more that we are all here on this planet for such a short time and life must continue. There must have been life before and there must be life after we die. But I was challenged to find out how that translated into the language of humans. I found myself wanting to serve. I felt there was a reason I was here."

After doing undergraduate work in nursing, which she subsequently felt ill-suited her, Sherry's quest led her to study the spiritual aspects of healing at a Lutheran seminary in the mean streets of the South Side of Chicago.

"The nature of human suffering," she said, "seemed to deeply involve the spirit as much, or more so, than the body and mind. I really wanted to explore more in-depth the main thrust of why we are here, the spiritual reason for it. So I took courses at the seminary to start putting some of that together and found myself on a whole other track."

It was the mid-1960s, and, like many people in that time, Sherry became caught up in social issues, especially the Civil Rights movement. The Lutheran seminary, which consisted mainly of white males, relocated to Chicago's ghetto area in order to make a more meaningful outreach to the black community there.

"What was beginning to happen," Sherry said, "was that the seminarians were being knifed in the alley and otherwise threatened. We were told not to go out anywhere, not even the grocery store, unless we were in groups of like six to

SIGNS AND SYMBOLS OF THE SECOND COMING

twelve. Truly, we were almost the only whites in the area, and that was extremely dangerous."

Sherry was tapped by the seminary leadership and put on staff as a mediator between the seminary and the community. Her task was to help build a bridge of understanding and to address the seminary's declaration that the South Side of Chicago was to offer the students a better and more comprehensive training as ministers, educators and counselors, through directly working with and for the needs of the community. Sherry's outlined plan to get back on track in addressing the issues at hand was adopted and she was put in charge. In the process, she worked hand-in-hand with Martin Luther King, Jr. and Jesse Jackson, among others.

"Martin Luther King had such an aura around him," Sherry said, "and never did I ever see anything other than that he lived his message."

Sherry was eventually ordained as a Baptist minister, since at the time the Lutheran Church did not permit the ordination of women.

NOT THE BOOGIE-MEN

Having sketched in a good portion of Sherry's religious history, there is also the matter of her encounters with the alien abductors.

"I had a dream as a child," she said, "that used to scare me. When I was a toddler, my mother or my grandma would come and find me screaming, in the middle of the night, that lights were coming at me. That's all I could explain. The lights were in different geometrical shapes. Sometimes I would be aware enough to feel that the lights had a kind of pressure and weight to them, and at times I couldn't breathe and felt like the weight and pressure would crush me.

"There aren't words," she continued, "when you're three years old, to explain to your family, that is so concerned, when your dreams are as unconventional as mine were — of lights and geometrical shapes — not boogie-men."

When the movie "2001: A Space Odyssey" was released in 1968, Sherry found a direct link to her childhood "dreams."

"It was like an angel just whirled everything around me," she said, "and everything made sense. That trip through space in the movie, when they were breaking the time barrier, the light barrier, in the spaceship, there is a rush like traveling through a light show. I'm sure you can identify the scene. That's exactly what I used to experience and feel when I was little."

Sherry grew up to find her soul mate in Brad Steiger, and the two were married on the Harmonic Convergence in 1987. They have collaborated as research-

SIGNS AND SYMBOLS OF THE SECOND COMING

ers and authors ever since and produced many books together on paranormal and religious subjects.

ON ANGELS AND BURIED EVIDENCE

Obviously, Sherry's credentials in religious and UFO terms are excellent. The conversation then shifted to her feelings about the translation problems sometimes encountered in the study of Biblical texts and how some things may be intended to remain mysteries forever.

"In some of the translations," she said, "with some of the words that we may have confused in Biblical translations from the ancient Hebrew, and with some of the things that may have been burned or books that have been banished, because we may not be meant to know what they contain, it all might have to do with travelers from other dimensions. It could have to do with ancient astronauts. It could have to do with angels on many levels. Or life and inner-life experiences on many levels. I'm not sure that we are to come to know all that exists in that realm because many people can't handle it."

Before meeting Brad, Sherry traveled widely, studying the teachings and beliefs of other cultures, including Native American shamans. It was no surprise to her that, after joining forces with Brad, their research together into the ancient mysteries of spiritual locations, including Peru, uncovered evidence of highly advanced cultures and teachings in newly discovered artifacts.

"There may be a vast amount of buried civilizations and undiscovered artifacts under the oceans, sands and lands of the world," she said, "that will bridge us together and demonstrate that we truly are one. In essence, I think I have learned from people like Rolling Thunder or Hopi Grandfather David that the Native-Americans also believe that there is something like a kind of Second Coming, and that we are going to go through a great transformation and cleansing on our planet.

"So I do believe," she continued, "in the Second Coming aspect. And I do believe that the parts of the Bible that used to turn me off and I would get upset about are now things to read and understand in a more complete way. Many of the root words which the translations come from are words that embrace a holistic kind of meaning. It is nearly impossible to single out one single word as the sole meaning from a whole list of possibilities. Often the meaning of a single word can embrace all of them as aspects of a total meaning.

"It is lost in translation," Sherry said, "and the focus of the meaning can be vastly different. We humans are sometimes so literal that we don't see the big picture of how they all fit together. I think there is a way to understand our universal connectedness and oneness in life through our individual transcendent expe-

SIGNS AND SYMBOLS OF THE SECOND COMING

riences. We have limited what are truly infinite teachings to our own finite human interpretations, rather than embrace them as a hologram for life. Our narrow definitions that become strict and demanding dogma, that there cannot be but one way and one method, have only led to unending division, alienation and wars."

Sherry continued to elaborate on workshops and presentations she has created.

"I put together programs," she said, "called 'Celebrate Life,' in the 60s, and 'Sacred Journey Through the Nature of Life,' in the 80s, that take the audience through a personal experience that words alone can't convey. I've felt guided since the childhood experience of light and shapes to help others understand our connection with all life and spirit through sacred geometry, sacred design, sound, music, light — all tangible things that can reveal the underlying essence of life, commonly revealed in most all teachings and religions — but without the labels limiting them as Baptist, Lutheran, Catholic, Jewish, Muslim, Hindu and all the shades between.

"I think that we go through cycles, small cycles and large cycles, which interact in an intricate dance that goes through stages of chaos to achieve harmony. We probably are on the brink of something wonderful and something terrible, which is an illustration of what our lives are. From moment to moment, there is, at the same time, death and birth, destruction and creation. We are dwelling on a planet of polarities. Our struggle is to find the balance and walk in harmony as we never know when our end might be coming. Each day we are called to transform ourselves.

"I think that is what many of the warnings throughout all religions say. In Christianity, of course, it's repent and be born again, which is the fundamental way of saying you're missing the mark. In Hebrew, 'clayey' — the word for 'sin' — includes the idea of something that is muddy or missing the mark. It's clear that our present-day world is muddied up, if you will, and we have missed the mark of perfect creation as it was once and is intended to be. The word 'repent' comes from the Greek word 'metanoia,' which literally means 'change your mind, change your direction.' It becomes less intimidating to think of Jesus' admonition of 'repent and sin no more' as being eternally appropriate. To paraphrase: Look, things are all muddied up and you've missed the point. Redirect your aim to the right mark and be clear."

THE MESSAGE IS THE SAME

"So we see," Sherry said, "that all the different religions are basically saying the same thing, and many of the teachings that Jesus spoke are almost identical to other ancient religions. I elaborate on this in my book, 'The Power of Prayer.'

SIGNS AND SYMBOLS OF THE SECOND COMING

There is a red thread of truth that runs through each of them to embroider a beautiful tapestry of a God without limit or definition. I believe they all teach us — in simplicity and in depth — that we should not judge one another, but love one another, and to realize our individual responsibility for every thought, word, action and deed, as it all has an effect on life all around us."

Sherry described the leader and elder in the Hopi tribe named Grandfather David, who guided his people to follow the ancient teachings of the Hopis.

"They are not to take any electricity," Sherry said, "and not to experience any of the technology of modem man. They literally grow all their own food in the harshness of the Upper Mesa in Northern Arizona. They carry their water. They do prayer, they do ceremonies, because they believe they are the guardians, the 'spirit holders,' of the North American continent. When Brad and I went to Peru, we saw the same thing. There's a group of Indians there who also refuse to take technology because they were told by — and they point up to the stars. Their belief is that angels from the sky told them not to embrace any new technology or to interact with outsiders that might corrupt their young ones and entice them into the materialistic toys of the world. They're almost identical in their beliefs to the ancient Hopis.

"They believe," she continued, "that if they maintain the ways that have been taught by their ancestors of love, of caring for one another, that their ancestors will return for them. For many of the Native-American tribes, they're called 'Star Gods,' and it is said they will return in 'baskets' to take the faithful back to their home in the sky. So in essence, I think that all of these things are expressing the same idea.

"We have to identify within ourselves the often suppressed thoughts that we have, thoughts that might be of anger, jealousy or hatred, that might lead us to inhumanity towards ourselves, towards our brothers, towards our neighbors. We must also look at the outer aspects, how everything we do in life has an effect. Every action has a reaction. All of that is what all the sacred teachings have taught. Examine the love and be caretakers of the greatness that we've been given."

One should not strain overmuch with the burden of proof, however.

"There is no way that any of us," Sherry said, "can prove that there is an existence beyond what we know of right now. We can't prove that we have love in our hearts. We can't prove that we love somebody. But in that same regard, I don't believe that we can prove that there's going to be a Second Coming, literally, in the way that so many — it's growing in numbers — believe is going to happen."

SIGNS AND SYMBOLS OF THE SECOND COMING
LORD JESUS COME

Sherry also responded to the question in which all the interviewees were asked for their thoughts on Jesus' declaration that some of those standing there with him would not taste death before the Coming of the Kingdom.

"He appeared to mean, 'I will come now. I will return immediately for you,'" Sherry said. "I believe that there may have been some translation problems. But there is an interesting word, 'Maranatha,' a word you may have heard of. Maranatha is a very common expression in churches and it literally comes from an ancient Aramaic word, the language of Jesus, and it means, 'Lord Jesus, come.' It's a petition to come, be with us, Lord. They used that all the time."

But there may be some degree of confusion caused by the quality of the messengers who delivered the news of the coming Kingdom.

"I believe that the disciples did believe," Sherry said, "that Jesus was going to come back immediately. Some of the ancient mysteries show us that there have been beings we call angels that could have been ancient astronauts and ancient astronauts we call angels. Some of them may not have been so great. Some of them may have served as messengers and they may have taught us how to use language and technology. Just as on Earth, we have positives and negatives, a blend of the light and the dark. I believe that the same thing exists in other realms and dimensions or aspects of life 'out there' — good angels, fallen angels, good ancient visitors and malevolent visitors. The tough part is discerning the good from the bad and all shades in between.

"They may have been more intelligent," she continued, "and may have interfered with our development using their advanced knowledge of genetics and DNA splicing, thereby altering our evolution on Planet Earth. Whether this was a good thing or a bad thing we could discuss ad infinitum, but there may be a universal dictum as is found in the popular television series 'Star Trek,' that it is forbidden to interfere with the evolution of another.

"There are a whole lot of theories about how life evolved, where we came from, and they may each be a piece of a giant jigsaw puzzle of life on Planet Earth and elsewhere. They truly are of vast importance, yet it all still remains a true mystery. Why are we here? What is the purpose of life? What happens when we die? It all seems crucial to our burning desire to know, to understand, but in essence the understanding comes more from the soul and inner guidance than it ever will from actual scientific, physical or historical proof. Perhaps it is meant to be a mystery to wonder and marvel over, not a problem to solve."

SIGNS AND SYMBOLS OF THE SECOND COMING
THE MARK OF THE BEAST

While Sherry obviously does not toe any kind of fundamentalist line of doctrine and believe literally in every prediction made in the Book of Revelation, she does concede that she's fascinated by one of the happenings prophesied in its pages.

"The Book of Revelation is a troublesome book," she said, "for a lot of people, but I find in it, and always have, some very intriguing things that baffle me. I've always wondered about the part where it says, 'You cannot buy or sell.'"

As background, Sherry told of one of the aspects of The Butterfly Center For Transformation, a nonprofit school she founded in the early seventies. The Life Craft part of the school was about helping people to learn to do things for themselves again and not be dependent on technology for every little daily need in life.

"Learn how to make your own clothes," she said, "to grow food, and not be so technologically evolved, so that if something should happen where we have no power, no electricity, or that everything begins to be taken from us, that we can be self-sufficient. The more I learned from Native-American shamans about not depending on technology, and considering that perhaps it was technology that destroyed Atlantis . . .

"So the part where Revelation says the day will come when you cannot buy or sell anything without the mark of the beast on your hand or forehead — this has somehow rung in my ears from the time I was little. I guess I had an intuition of what this might mean."

Sherry said that in the 1970s, she worked as a head writer for an advertising agency at the same time she was trying to get her classes off the ground. She was asked to work up an ad campaign for the very first bank machine.

"You know, where you drive through the teller," she explained, "and you have a card and the card has a number and a magnetic strip. When I saw that, it just went 'beep, beep, beep.' It was like that part in Revelation. I started noticing in the grocery store that there were these straight lines, thick and thin, that began to appear on some products, and that we now know as the product code. I kept asking people, what are those? What is that number? What are those lines? It started to appear on more and more products until now you know you can't buy anything that does not have the product code. You can't sell anything unless it has a product code."

Sherry wondered how the Book of Revelation could carry off such an obvious "hit" and actually predict the future accurately.

SIGNS AND SYMBOLS OF THE SECOND COMING

"How in the Book of Revelation is that possible?" she asked. "That that would be a sign to look for? The more research I did, the more I came to think that there are certain signs that forewarn those who have ears to listen about some major changes that will come about. They've happened before and they're going to happen again. We can learn to live within it. We can warn others. We can figure out what that means for us. I think perhaps it might have happened before, where technology evolved to the point where the abuse and misuse of it destroyed the world. There seems to me to be a cosmic combination of a kind of 'predetermination,' predetermined outer cycle occurrences, which we have little or no control over, and a kind of 'free will' within smaller cycles that we can do something about in choosing how we deal with things. They each affect the other in the micro and macro cosmos of our lives."

RETURNING TO PERFECTION

Sherry was asked if she entertained any notions of a perfect, post-Second Coming world.

"It couldn't happen," she said, "unless everybody had an enlightenment and a total awareness in the same instant for us to return to Eden, if us means all of us, all souls on Earth. I do believe it's possible, but I think it has to come from each individual. Although there are so many mysteries throughout history that do happen in an instant. It's both allegorical and physical."

Sherry talked about the symbol of the UFO as the technological manifestation of the way we yearn for something coming from out there to rescue us and save us.

"Many people talk about an avatar coming," she said, "or the Ashtar Command coming, or a giant spaceship coming to bring Eden back to Earth or to be the New Jerusalem. There's a part of every one of us that wants to go back to perfection. We want a rebirthing to innocence and renewal.

"I think we're always going to be searching," she continued, "and perhaps it is possible to go back or to achieve an Eden-like state of existence. But when you look at the way things are now, sometimes it's easy for people who are sensitive to get very depressed, because it doesn't seem like we've really evolved that much. We're still going through the same issues and we're still saying 'me and mine' and 'mine is better than yours,' and 'you have to do it my way,' or 'we have to have a line around this and a line around that,' separating ourselves, our country, our religions.

"I believe there are powers and principalities, as stated in the Bible, and that there are negative spirits, negative energies, positive energies, and there's

SIGNS AND SYMBOLS OF THE SECOND COMING

some kind of divine interaction between all of it. All of it can be addressed as something that helps us grow and learn and become better. But obviously there are some negative things that many people or spirits or souls or entities choose not to advance beyond.

"And sometimes it seems like the separation or the chasm," Sherry went on, "is even deeper and stronger and larger than ever, which is part of prophecy, that there will be wars and rumors of wars. Almost all the prophecies that I have read or heard people tell about in other languages through translators say the same thing. That just before, there is a great cleansing of the Earth. Whether it's from the Native-American perspective or the return of Jesus from the fundamentalist perspective, they're all saying that there will be an extremely difficult time ahead of us, and the signs point to soon, where plagues, diseases, wars, earth changes and upheaval will result in great despair at the death and destruction.

"So get ready," she said. "Repent. Change your mind. Change your direction. Become a good person now. This may be the last breath you take. Perhaps, with a unity of hearts and minds, we could have prevented these extreme cycles from occurring and maybe our global outlook would be more positive and whole. But by not heeding the admonitions and teachings of the eons, we might have to brace ourselves for what could be coming. One of the most important things to me for whatever comes next is to know that the path to God is through love, and love has no boundaries and no limit to its definition."

SIGNS AND SYMBOLS OF THE SECOND COMING

CHAPTER EIGHT

A WORLDWIDE SPIRITUAL AWAKENING

Is it possible to know today, this very moment, the identity of the true antichrist? Read what Dr. Frank Stranges has to say on the subject. His answer may surprise you.

Does a more accurate translation of the verse in which Christ says, "In my father's house there are many mansions," imply that we are intended to take up residence on various planets throughout the universe? Will certain of the Chosen be dispatched to serve as rulers on other worlds?

What kind of glorious blessing may await the faithful in the Last Days, just before the antichrist takes power? Will humanity at last know love and caring for one another as the clock winds down toward the Great Tribulation?

Dr. Frank Stranges is a well-known author and researcher whose books include "Stranger at the Pentagon," "Millennium Seven," and "Out-Waiting Tomorrow," all of which have been translated into many languages and sold throughout

SIGNS AND SYMBOLS OF THE SECOND COMING

the world. Stranges was born and raised in Brooklyn, New York. He attended Eastern Bible College in Pennsylvania and later graduated from North Central Seminary in Minneapolis, Minnesota.

"I became interested in the Bible," Stranges said, "at a very young age and started preaching at the age of thirteen."

Stranges' interest in UFOs began in 1945, while attending Bible College.

"My ex-roommate," he said, "was a United States Marine pilot and he told me a story during the first few days of school. Everybody was swapping yarns about what they did when they were younger or when they were in military service. He was a United States Marine at the time, leading a squadron of planes. The planes were suddenly buzzed by three disc-shaped objects. Naturally, the pilots broke formation and then regrouped. This happened three times. The third time, the commanding officer told them to return the ships to base, which they did."

Next came the familiar tale of military UFO witnesses being ordered to keep silent by their higher-ups.

"They were gathered in a boardroom," Stranges said, "and they were told, they weren't asked what they saw, they were told that what they saw was a flight of highflying Canadian geese. Well, these things looked like inverted saucers, and my roommate said these were certainly not geese. So he raised his hand and before he got two words out of his mouth, the commanding officer said, 'Look, Brown, keep your mouth shut. What you saw was Canadian flying geese. That's it. Period. Case closed. Dismissed.' So I went as far as to get the names and addresses of the other pilots, who fortunately lived in New York, New Jersey and Pennsylvania. I took my entire summer vacation period to meet these people and I got their stories.

"Every one of their stories," Stranges said, "checked out perfectly. And that's what got me started on the UFO phenomenon, way back in 1945."

BACK TO THE ORIGINAL LANGUAGES

Stranges is clearly a seasoned expert in both religion and the study of UFOs. His response to the initial question about the Second Coming also displayed his command of ancient languages.

"First of all," he said, "in order to understand properly any Biblical passage at all, there's a tremendous value in having a background in the original languages. I have found in my personal experience that many ministers are too lazy to do research into the actual languages that Christ spoke and that Saint Paul and Moses spoke. The reality is that these ancient languages, which I studied in Bible Col-

SIGNS AND SYMBOLS OF THE SECOND COMING

lege and seminary — Aramaic, Greek and Hebrew — contain a wealth of information about the meaning of some of the words that were spoken and written in those days.

"Anyone who would even attempt," he continued, "to interpret Biblical passages would have to agree that they'd want to go to the source, to the actual original languages. Now, over a period of hundreds, even thousands of years, stories have been handed down from one to scribe to another in foreign languages. And as these languages, including the Aramaic, were translated into the Hebrew and then into the Greek and then into English, there was an awful lot lost in the translation. For that reason, you've got many misinterpretations of the scriptures. I hear them every day on religious radio and television.

"For instance," he said, "Christ never did say on the cross, 'My God, why hast thou forsaken me?' He never uttered those words. The spoken language of Christ in that day was pure Aramaic, and what he said from the cross in the Aramaic language was, 'This is the day. This is the time that I have been waiting to fulfill, and I have fulfilled it.' Now, that's a far cry from 'Father, why hast thou forsaken me?'"

Stranges talked about another mistranslated Biblical passage, one that is particularly important to him.

"There is a passage in the New Testament," he said, "which gives rise to the idea of life in outer space and life on other planets. Christ said, in the King James 1611 version, 'In my father's house are many mansions.' He didn't say that at all. He said, 'In my father's universe are many dwelling places.' Well, you won't hear that at the Baptist Church next Sunday morning, I'm sure. But you see it lends credibility to the space sciences. It addresses itself to the possibility of life on other planets."

WE'RE LIVING IN THE LAST DAYS

"Many preachers have preached," Stranges said, "as though the Lord Jesus Christ was going to come tomorrow. They use scare tactics to actually frighten their listeners, which is a bunch of garbage."

He next began to recite statistics on earthquakes, pestilence, famine, warfare, abrupt changes in the normal weather patterns — the list went on and on.

"Now these are definitely points," he said, "that can be placed in the category of the Last Days. We're living in the Last Times. And as these things continue, we're going to find more and more that we're going to be getting closer to the Coming of the Lord Jesus Christ. But something is going to happen before the Second Coming. Something tremendous. Something that will bless the members

SIGNS AND SYMBOLS OF THE SECOND COMING

of the human race such as nothing ever has before.

"That is, before the Second Coming," he continued, "and I prophesied this in many of my church sermons, we are going to witness a worldwide spiritual awakening. Not a religious awakening, mind you. It's going to be a worldwide spiritual awakening that's going to reach across denominations and religions throughout the entire planet."

It is only after that spiritual blessing that the more evil times will come, according to Stranges.

"Following that great revival," he said, "of spirituality and people beginning to love each other and trust each other as never before, then there's going to be a short period of devastation and then the End Time is going to come."

Stranges goes so far as to name the person he thinks will be the antichrist, the Man of Sin, whose number is 666.

"This old boy, he lives up in Iran right now," Stranges declared. "We've traced his lineage right back to the very beginning. He's going to put in an appearance but he will not take office. He will not take authority on Planet Earth until the church has been taken out, when the believers, those who believe in Christ, will be taken up. They'll be changed in the twinkling of an eye. It will be a tremendous day when the Second Coming takes place. And immediately following the Second Coming, you're going to see the revelation of he who is called the Man of Sin, Number 666, and he's to create laws that will make it so difficult for the people who remain.

"And the people who remain," Stranges continued, "are going to be forced by law to take his mark, in the palm of their right hand or else in their forehead, if not both. And unless they have that mark, they won't be able to cash a check, they won't be able to buy a loaf of bread or ride in any transportation that you have to pay for. And then, following that a short season, the people are going to be so persecuted that they're going to wonder why they didn't believe in Christ in the first place and escape all this devastation.

"His reign is going to be very short on this planet. We're looking at about three and a half years. And then the return of Christ with his people, with his 'saints,' as the Aramaic calls them, with his followers, with his believers. They are going to return to this Earth, and Almighty God is going to judge mankind according to the deeds performed in the flesh.

"In other words, if you've done wrong, you're going to have to pay for it. You're going to have to pay the piper. And this is going to bring in the literal kingdom of God on Earth, following the Great Tribulation Period, following the great

SIGNS AND SYMBOLS OF THE SECOND COMING

time when God's people come back to Earth with Him to judge the nations. And after that, there's going to be peace on Earth, which is written in the final chapter of the Book of Revelation, a time in which there will be no sorrow, no sickness, no corruption, no sin, no foulness of any shape, size or color."

NAMING THE ANTICHRIST

After that impressive, almost dizzying capsule description of what Stranges believes will happen in the Last Days, the question was asked, just who is this antichrist that Stranges goes so far as to name publicly?

"He is a royal prince," Stranges answered. "His name is Prince Abdul Berraba Baha. He was born in Mecca, the holy city of the Mohammedans, out of wedlock. His father, Abdul Hammid the Second, was a notorious murderer. The prince is a member of the Bahai religion. I've traced his lineage clear back to 2000 B.C., right back to Abraham."

There has of course been a long history of failed attempts to name the antichrist down through the ages, and if Stranges turns out to be right, it's not the kind of thing where one would get much satisfaction in saying, "I told you so." But it is included here to bear witness to what Stranges believed at the time this interview was conducted.

DOES THE BIBLE SPEAK OF THE INNER EARTH?

Stranges believes that there is some form of life under the Earth that is going to be equally blessed by the coming of the Kingdom of God.

"There's a funny word in the Aramaic language," he explained, "which also testifies that there's going to be life on Earth that's going to be blessed, as well as life under the Earth. It also says in one of the Gospels that 'every knee shall bow and every tongue shall confess him,' meaning of those in the heavens, of those on the Earth, and of those under the Earth. This is very significant, and it lends a lot of credibility to the theory of life on the inside of this planet."

RULING WITH GOD

There are other precious rewards that Stranges believes are promised to the faithful.

"Well, when that final time comes," he said, "and God hands out his rewards, he said he's going to give us the privilege of ruling and reigning with him. Well,

SIGNS AND SYMBOLS OF THE SECOND COMING

common sense tells you that we're not going to rule and reign over each other. So with the gifts that he's going to be giving people, and the appointments he's going to make, certain individuals, I believe, will be dispatched throughout the universe to other populated planets.

"Not that these people need a savior, but they're going to need a ruler. They're going to need someone to guide and direct them. And who better than those who have accepted Christ, who have given themselves over to the Lord one hundred percent, and who will be entrusted with the authority and the power to rule and reign in His place on these other planets?

"And with that," Stranges said, "I say an amen."

SIGNS AND SYMBOLS OF THE SECOND COMING

CHAPTER NINE

SIGNS TO WATCH FOR

There is no way of knowing, if one is honest, when or even if the Second Coming will ever take place. But it is possible to be observant of the current times and seasons and to be on guard against the many deceptions that can so easily ensnare even the most sincere of believers.

IS THAT A HOLOGRAM I SEE?

One potential deception would boggle the mind of even the most hardened students of the paranormal as well as current conspiracy theorists: the use of holograms projected in the sky to create the illusion of the Second Coming as a mass invasion from outer space. It's not a joke. Many believe that the technology already exists.

Well-known UFO reporter, Scott Corrales, writing in the March 2003 issue of "FATE Magazine," described an incident said to have occurred in Cuba that makes the idea of a false Second Coming more than plausible.

"It has been possible," Corrales wrote, "to manufacture heavenly supernatural images for quite some time, and these can be employed to manipulate people into believing certain ideas, and, perhaps more importantly, to reinforce loyalties.

"One such case," Corrales continued, "dates back to 1982, when hundreds of Cubans taking their nightly walk along the seaside promenade known as the Malecon witnessed a sudden flash over Havana Bay, which immediately made them suspect that they were under attack. But bombs did not rain out of the sky; instead, there was an overwhelming brightness which gradually coalesced into an image of the Blessed Virgin — more specifically Cuba's patroness, la Caridad del Cobre — extending her arms toward the startled masses on the promenade as she remained suspended in the night sky. Unlike traditional images of the

SIGNS AND SYMBOLS OF THE SECOND COMING

Blessed Virgin, this one did not bear the Christ-child in her arms, nor were there any other religious items such as crosses associated with it. The divine protector appeared to be wearing a snow-white mantle that contrasted brightly against the prevailing darkness."

Corrales goes on to say that Cuban authorities tried to cover up the strange events, but word of what had happened still managed to leak out through a couple of Miami radio stations. The divine image was again seen days later at the port of Mariel, and this time soldiers opened up with machine-guns in an attempt to blast the vision out of the sky. One of the soldiers later required psychiatric treatment.

In the aftermath, it was suggested that a U.S. Navy submarine had projected "an advanced holographic image as part of psychological warfare operations against the Cuban government."

"Hard though it may be to believe," Corrales wrote, "in both the sophistication of such techniques and the fact that their use would ever be authorized, the fact remains that it would not be the only one — albeit it was the most spectacular — ever employed against Cuba's socialist regime."

One is reminded of the exploding cigar plot once considered by the late President Richard Nixon as a way to assassinate the irksome Fidel Castro. The attempt to use holography is more sophisticated indeed.

PROJECT BLUE BEAM

The holography psychological warfare operation Corrales is describing is often referred to as Project Blue Beam. One can find mention of it all over the Internet, where rumors of a "technologically simulated" Second Coming are rampant.

According to one Internet author, David Openheimer, "The 'system' has already been tested. Holographic projections of the 'Christ Image' have already been seen in some remote desert areas. These sightings have only been reported in tabloid newspapers, so they are instantly rendered moot. They can also project images of alien craft, aliens, monsters, angels — you name it. Computers will coordinate the satellites and software will run the show-and-tell.

"Specifically," Openheimer continued, "the 'show' will consist of multiple holographic images projected to different parts of the planet, each receiving different images according to the predominating religious faith. Not a single area will be excluded. With computer animation and sound effects appearing to come from the depths of space, astonished followers of the various creeds will witness their own returned Messiah in spectacularly convincing, lifelike realness. Naturally, this superbly staged, full-scale production will result in social and religious

SIGNS AND SYMBOLS OF THE SECOND COMING

disorder on a massive scale."

The mind reels when forced to consider that a make-believe Second Coming could deceive virtually everyone on this planet and that the technology to carry out such a wicked masquerade already exists.

CHECKLIST OF DOOM

At the close of the interview with Gary Stearman of "Prophecy in the News," Stearman offered a checklist of events to watch for as the clock winds down to our potential annihilation.

Watch for the rise of world socialism.

Watch for the rise of apostasy and open denial of Biblical truth, that is, the kind of truth that believes that the Bible literally speaks of events to come.

Watch for the rise of moral chaos, and with that moral chaos the open hatred of those who worship the Lord.

Watch for the rise of spiritism and belief in demons.

Watch Jerusalem, because it's the center of religious controversy for the world — Arabs, Christians and Jews. All desire to make that the center of their plans.

Watch for an incredible event in which millions disappear in a single day as the Church is taken home. And at that point, watch for the rise of unbridled evil as the rule of the Holy Spirit is ended upon Earth.

If you are a political observer, part of the checklist would include the establishment of an increasingly powerful United Nations that literally has the power of judicial judgment.

Watch for the rise of an international world market that becomes so powerful it controls all markets.

Watch for wars in the Middle East, and for oil blackmail, and for energy battles to be kicked off, because the Book of Revelation says that oil will be a great bone of contention in the Latter Days.

Watch for someone, probably from Europe or in the Mediterranean area, to stand up and become a very powerful world leader. This man may attempt to bring the peoples of the Earth together. He's going to be very talented, a very gifted speaker, an attractive personality, and ultimately he'll display power. He's going to be the antichrist.

One of the big things to watch for is an invasion by the Russian army into the

SIGNS AND SYMBOLS OF THE SECOND COMING

Middle East. We have the United States in Iraq, which is the power center of the Middle East, and it wouldn't take much for that Russian invasion to happen, even as the Bible predicts.

THE TIME IS AS YET UNKNOWN

Admittedly, not everyone interviewed for this book would agree with Stearman's assessment of the future. This terrible era of dread Stearman lays out could pass us by completely. It is only the passage of time itself that is the true revelator.

If there can be said to be any single point of agreement existing between the various experts who speak in this volume, it would probably be that the whole issue of the Second Coming remains largely hidden behind the proverbial clouds of heaven. One can easily draw the conclusion that any one of the scenarios described herein could eventually prove to be the truth.

And as Brad and Sherry Steiger so eloquently warned, we should live as though each and every day was Judgment Day and discipline ourselves accordingly. Whether Jesus ever returns or not, such a moral and loving approach to daily living surly couldn't hurt.

SIGNS AND SYMBOLS OF THE SECOND COMING

SIGNS AND SYMBOLS OF THE SECOND COMING

THE VISITATION

MODERN MIRACLES AND SIGNS

By Timothy Green Beckley

SIGNS AND WONDERS

Those who realize that our days are numbered, that we are living in the "End Times," will have no trouble accepting the information which we have gathered and are hereby presenting for the first time. Spiritual leaders, Biblical students, as well as New Age leaders all agree that our planet is going through a critical phase and that one "wrong move" could be the end of civilization as we have come to know it.

We have been informed that in the "Last Days" there will be many signs and wonders which will appear all around us. These signs and wonders will take many forms and will serve as a warning that we had better get all our affairs in order. All over our planet, people are becoming more aware of the situation. Small groups have recently formed to exchange information and to try and build up hope. These are people of all different religious backgrounds and beliefs.

In this special report, I have tried to present only a small sample of all the evidence which is freely available and which indicates that GREAT CHANGES are on the horizon. This information, which has come from various sources, is proof that the Day of Revelation can not be far off. From the four corners of the Earth, a female archetypal figure is being observed by the holy and the unholy alike. At the same time, a Christ-like apparition has also materialized many, many times. Signs and wonders in the sky are also increasing as crosses have formed in front

SIGNS AND SYMBOLS OF THE SECOND COMING

of multitudes, not to even mention the "Fiery Chariots" and "Wheels within Wheels" which have become popularly known as UFOs or flying saucers.

It is not our purpose in THE VISITATION to try and explain the meaning or purpose of what is happening. Our goal is merely to show proof that something truly dramatic is transpiring all around us. For the most part such occurrences have been kept out of the newspapers and off the television screen. There is a general feeling that, if the facts were made known, people would panic and our civilization would crumble. My feeling is that society doesn't need any help in that direction, that the very fiber of our culture is about to give way at any moment as it is. It stands to reason that we should try and analyze what is being placed before us. We owe it to ourselves to get down to the bottom of this mystery. It appears that our lives are about to be altered, that some super-intelligence is trying to warn us of impending danger. If it doesn't open our eyes (the signs, as we shall see, are all around us), and expand our way of thinking, it may be too late to do anything about this rapidly worsening situation.

THE VIRGIN IN PUERTO RICO

Recently, we received a sensational set of clippings from a close friend in Altamesa, Puerto Rico. Mr. A. Rodriguez, Jr. was kind enough to mail us the stories as they were printed in the February 10th, 11th and 13th edition of EL VOCERO. Since the material was in Spanish, we gave the clippings over to Carol Rodriguez (no relation) of Queens, N.Y., who did the translations for us. As you read about the apparition of the Virgin, it will become obvious that the children involved have related the experiences as they happened to them. Being from a Catholic background, it is only natural that they would think of the woman in terms of the Virgin Mary. Let us read these accounts and then we shall continue with even more startling disclosures.

CHILDREN SEE IMAGES OF THE VIRGIN

Hundreds of spectators invaded 7th Street, Hill Brothers at Rio Piedra to catch a glimpse of the alleged Miraculous Virgin, which rose up from a palm tree in the yard of a private family residence.

While many of the curious knelt and prayed, others remained silent, staring towards the location of the alleged apparition. "The Virgin has been there since last Thursday night," said a nervous high school student, who would not identify himself.

Seven children from the "Villa Capri" elementary school of the Parielas Hill Brothers were the first ones to report the alleged apparition of the Virgin. Twelve-year-old Cristina Flamer told "El Vocero" that at about 8:30 P.M. last Thursday,

SIGNS AND SYMBOLS OF THE SECOND COMING

she was under a mango tree, conversing with her school friends, Luis Sepulveda, 12, Augelita Caballeri, 10, Luz Irene Pagan, 12, David Azola, 11, Connie Gonzales, 14 and others. She heard a soft feminine voice calling her. "I could hear it very clearly saying: 'Look at me, my daughter, look at me.' Then I looked over there and in back of that house, against the palm tree, I saw the figure of a woman which gradually appeared, first taking the form of a nun and then that of the Virgin. My friends also saw her. And she is still there." The girl pointed towards the location of the supposed apparition. At that moment, Eddie Deese, the photographer who accompanied me, and myself were able to observe, against the palm tree, what gave the impression of being an image of the Virgin.

"After seeing her for the first time," the girl continued to narrate, "I was able to observe when the Virgin rose, like this, with her arms open, looking straight at us. Then I knelt down to pray. One of my friends suffered an attack of nerves."

From another source, an elderly neighbor in the area exclaimed, in between sobs, "The end of the world is coming. We must all pray and repent. This must certainly be a warning from the Miraculous Virgin that we must prepare ourselves for the coming of the Son of God."

Another neighbor who also alleges having seen the Virgin was Rafael Betancourt, a transporter of heavy equipment and a resident of 11th Street. "The Apparition has been manifesting since last Thursday night and disappearing towards dawn. From here you also can see that we are telling the truth. Look in that direction towards that palm tree. There you can see the image of the Virgin," he exclaimed, nervously pointing towards the palm tree.

A few seconds later, a parish priest arrived on the scene, along with the clergy of various other churches, to collaborate the alleged apparition of the Virgin. Patrol cars from the precinct of Monte Hatillo also arrived and began questioning those who claimed to have seen the image.

SIGNS AND SYMBOLS OF THE SECOND COMING

The children who first witnessed the miracle told a reporter what it is they saw. Published accounts say that it was impossible to break down their story. All those who spoke with the children personally agreed that they were telling the truth.

HUNDREDS GO TO SEE THE VIRGIN

Yesterday, an avalanche of curiosity seekers continued pouring into 7th Street at Parcelos Hill Brothers, Rio Piedras, to see the apparition of the Virgin which allegedly rose up against a palm tree in the backyard of a private residence.

A number of children had seen the image last Thursday night, but it was not until yesterday that they made public their revelations. "I told my mama, but I didn't dare tell anyone else, because I was afraid," said a little girl of about ten.

Twelve-year-old Cristina Flamer, a fifth grade student at the Villa Capri elementary school, situated right on Parcelos, said she heard the Virgin call her saying, "Look at me, my daughter. Look at me."

"I looked to see who was calling me and when I looked over there, where that palm tree is, I saw the body of a woman gradually forming as a nun. Later I saw it become the Virgin in a long dress." She saw the Virgin rise several feet in the air from the palm tree with open arms. "I saw her very clearly; it was the Virgin," reaffirmed the child.

While Cristina related the story, the other children involved, Luis Sepulveda, Angelita Caballeri, Luz Irene Pagan, David Azola and Connie Gonzalez, all gathered around. Rafael Betancourt collaborated the children's story. "I also saw the image. There is no doubt that it looked like the Virgin."

SIGNS AND SYMBOLS OF THE SECOND COMING

Twelve-year-old Cristina Flamer (center) gets down on her knees as she recreates moments in her life she will never forget — when the "Blessed Mother" appeared to her and her friends. Skeptics soon turned into believers when they heard the story first hand.

THOUSANDS COME TO SEE THE VIRGIN

Since yesterday, close to 10,000 people have been to 7th Street, Parcelos Hill Brothers, Rio Piedras, to observe the apparition of the Virgin.

SIGNS AND SYMBOLS OF THE SECOND COMING

Fervent believers from all over the island continued to arrive in that area, anxious to prove the existence of the Virgin. Many of the curious brought with them tents and other camping gear and announced their intentions of keeping a vigil for as long as necessary in order to see the apparition.

There have been many priests and nuns arriving from outside of the area, some from the United States. One of the priests visited the home of Cristina Flamer. Holding up a crucifix, he asked the 5th grader, "Do you swear upon the cross of our savior Jesus Christ that you have seen the Virgin? Are you sure? You know that God could punish you if you lie."

"I am telling the truth. I swear it," responded the girl as she kissed the crucifix.

The mother of Lucy Garcia, one of the witnesses, expressed her faith. "Around here, there are many who are incredulous, but we remain calm in the knowledge that we have told the truth. I have seen the Virgin again tonight at about 8:30 P.M., but if you go to that spot right now and look in that direction, you would see a pretty large cross." This claim has been confirmed by other neighbors in the area.

The sisters, Connie, Cristina and Jeannette Gonzales, reaffirmed that they had seen the Virgin last Wednesday night. "She stood like this with her arms open, and later disappeared, leaving behind a cross," stated their brother, 11-year-old Michael, who also claimed to have seen the image.

The children's mother said that the other night when she went to bed, as she thought about the apparition of the Virgin, was it real or just an illusion, she heard a sweet voice say, "You should pray for your dear mother, who is ill."

"It gave me a tremendous shock, to receive definite proof that the voice which had spoken to me had been that of the Virgin. Early the next day, I went to the Industrial Hospital where my mother had been in critical condition, and, to my surprise, she was in a much improved condition." The young mother expressed herself with much emotion.

According to the story told by the people of this neighborhood, the Virgin has been appearing on this site since last Thursday.

"Sometimes she faces front as if she wants to come towards us, and at other times she turns her back or hides behind the branches of the palm tree." This is what they claim.

SIGNS AND SYMBOLS OF THE SECOND COMING

THE CAMERA DOES NOT TELL LIES! — HERE IS PHOTOGRAPHIC PROOF THAT THE "BLESSED MOTHER" DID APPEAR AS WITNESSES HAVE TESTIFIED. SHE APPEARED OVER A NEARBY HOUSE IN THE MIDDLE OF A PALM TREE. FIRST SHE WOULD STAND TO THE SIDE, AND THEN SHE WOULD FACE THE MULTITUDE WHO HAD COME TO SEE HER WITH THEIR OWN EYES.

UNUSUAL PHENOMENON IN THE SKY

In addition to the appearance of the Virgin, Puerto Rico also seems to be privileged when it comes to signs appearing in the heavens. This photo was taken in early 1981 over the south coast at noon. Those looking up at the sky caught a glimpse of something very strange around the sun. There was a brilliant, multicolored circle around the sun which lasted for two hours. Hundreds of people called the radio stations in and around the city of Ponce and thousands were out in the street watching the manifestation. The news agencies said that it was the most talked about event in many years in the second largest city in Puerto Rico. "I saw it!" said Sergeant Ismael Serrano, Chief of Police in Coano. "The sun was in a great circle of bright colors — green, orange, red, blue — and around that circle there was a golden border. It was beautiful. It was difficult to stop looking at it."

SIGNS AND SYMBOLS OF THE SECOND COMING

FAITH CAN MOVE MOUNTAINS

Recently we met an attractive actress at the home of a close friend and during the course of our conversation I happened to mention the fact that I was working on a paper containing the testimony of those who have reportedly seen visions of the Virgin Mary. The woman's eyes lit up. "It's funny you should mention that," she said, her voice lowered as she started to talk in total confidence. "You see, my husband is Jewish but he wears a necklace with the Virgin Mary around his neck." I asked her why, if he were not a Christian, he would do such a thing? "Well, when he was four years old, he was in a field and there was an opening in the clouds . . . and this woman came down and spoke to him." The actress said her husband, a well established Hollywood film director, could never remember the actual content of the message he was given, but he did feel the meeting was a positive one. "He told me the woman was quite attractive, and she seemed to

SIGNS AND SYMBOLS OF THE SECOND COMING

radiate love," the actress went on, but only after I promised not to reveal her or her husband's identity.

Indeed, it is not necessary to be a Christian to take part in such a miracle. In the volume, "Apparition Phenomenon Manifest At Zeitun, Cairo, Egypt," no less than seven Moslems confirmed the appearances of the "Blessed Mother." Striking photos of the materialization were widely circulated in non-Christian papers, and the event was even witnessed by a medical doctor, a man of rigid scientific background who would not normally believe in such things.

APPARITIONS IN THE U.S.S.R.

According to several sources, the Virgin Mary has been seen repeatedly in Russia, a country that is officially atheistic.

The first apparition is said to have occurred on July 13, 1962, in the Janovai Collectivized Zone, in Skiamonial, in Lithuania, one of the republics in the former U.S.S.R. An 18-year-old girl named Franzeska Ramova Macugs suddenly found herself surrounded by a strange light. Then she noticed a completely white altar on which there were six candles burning. She next saw the Blessed Virgin, who was dressed in white with a blue sash around her waist. The Virgin Mary had an expression of "suffering" on her face, and as she raised her arms in supplication she disappeared right in front of the teenager.

However, Franzeska was to see her again. The second time, the Virgin was standing on a white cloth which had small red crosses all over it. The Blessed Mother said to her: "You have been chosen because of your simplicity," and then added: "I cannot save men from destruction, if they will not return to God!"

An altar of white stones has been erected on the spot where the apparition first materialized. And though it has been destroyed over and over again by the Communist Youth Movement, it has been rebuilt by devotees time and time again.

The Virgin Mary is also said to have appeared in a similar manner in various other parts of the U.S.S.R., such as the cities of Rostov, Kharkhov and Leningrad. As can be expected, these visits by the "Queen of Heaven" have aroused a very active renewal in religious fervor. The seers are said to have declared: "The Mother of God is appearing in various parts of our fatherland in order to open our eyes. She wants us to pray more fervently so that the world may be saved from destruction."

One of the latest apparitions is said to have taken place in a village called Tombow, which is only 25 miles south of Moscow. It was said that at some time in the future the Blessed Mother would appear in the capitol itself. Moreover, a large crowd is said to have witnessed the apparition of Our Lady when a "white hand"

SIGNS AND SYMBOLS OF THE SECOND COMING

appeared in the clear sky. The hand was holding a huge pen and wrote the following words:

THERE IS STILL MORE EVIL THAN GOOD IN THE WORLD! IT IS WINTER FOR MY PEOPLE! NOW IS THE TIME OF REPENTANCE. NO GOOD SOUL WILL BE LEFT AMONG THE EVIL ONES; AND NO EVIL SOUL WILL BE LEFT AMONG THE GOOD ONES. HEED MY WARNING. PRODUCE FRUITS OF REPENTANCE. I WILL SAVE THE GOD-FEARING. ACCEPT YOUR RESPONSIBILITIES. THE TIME IS VERY NEAR AT HAND. I WILL RETURN SOON.

AMEN.

It is said that the "hand" wrote for about half an hour. The writing could be seen by everyone all over the city. It could be read for three hours. Thus a great fear gripped the people who filled the streets, so that all the means of transport were paralyzed. Just imagine the uneasiness of the materialist leaders. Yet, from fear of provoking a mutiny, they did not dare arrest the onlookers who were thus able to pass the heavenly message to the ever increasing number of believers.

To say the least, this has caused all sorts of trouble.

The stories we have heard attest to the fact that the Kremlin leaders are at a loss as to how to stop the large number of conversions which have resulted after all these apparitions of the Virgin. They have tried various explanations. The latest explanation is so base that, in the eyes of the people, the stories the authorities tell are quite ridiculous.

For example, they have claimed that the apparitions have been manufactured by America. It is claimed that the CIA has managed to smuggle into Russia a beautiful spy from Washington or from Hollywood who can speak Russian without a foreign accent. Supposedly, the CIA has been able to make her appear in various parts of Russia in a beam of light produced by an advanced form of cine projector.

We are told that the Russian people are not falling for such an explanation, that they are clearly not so gullible as to believe such a fabrication. Faith in a Supreme Being and devotion to prayer has been spreading rapidly among the people, so much so that the KGB is said to be bitterly disappointed that it cannot send that "Virgin" either to a camp in Siberia or to a mental asylum, as it would be able to do with any other "real" enemy of the regime.

As time marches on, no doubt the visions will increase in number until they can be denied no longer. It is interesting to note that even a country where religion is officially frowned upon is not exempt to such manifestations. Probably there are many more "miracles" of a similar nature which have either gone unreported

SIGNS AND SYMBOLS OF THE SECOND COMING

or have not made it out from behind the "Iron Curtain."

Word has even reached us that photos do exist of these apparitions inside the Soviet Union. We are trying to obtain these pictures currently and should we be successful we will present them in a future edition of this special report.

THE "GREAT MOTHER'S" RETURN

Many atheists are among those to have seen apparitions of the "Great Mother." Carol Rodriguez went through a period in her life when she lacked faith. However, partly due to a strange series of events, the talented graphic artist became a convert to that which is of a mystical nature.

"I had been really depressed because one of my best friends had committed suicide," Carol said. "At the time, I considered myself an atheist, partly due to my Catholic upbringing, which had turned me off to organized religion. I didn't know what I was going to do with my life. I couldn't get a job and nothing seemed to be happening right for me."

One night while she was in bed, Carol had a very vivid vision which she finds difficult to believe was only a dream. "I saw myself going to the church where my parents used to send me twice a week. I walked into the church and saw the statue of the Virgin. I got on my knees in front of her and suddenly I felt great relief. Without warning, the face of the statue turned into a white light and a while later my life started to improve."

As time passed, Carol says she discovered that whenever she became extremely upset, something would happen and she would get an image of the Virgin Mary in her mind. "Other times I'd walked into a room and the radio would be on and it would be playing the Beatle song 'Let It Be,' with the lyrics about how in times of trouble and sorrow 'Mother Mary comes to me, speaking words of wisdom . . . Let it Be.'" On such occasions, Carol would almost always feel very uplifted.

Her most recent experience concerning Mother Mary happened just a few months ago.

"I wasn't getting enough sleep," she recalled, "because my job, which involves working with young children, was becoming very taxing. It felt like I was having a nervous breakdown. I would stay up crying into my pillow I was so disturbed. I started praying for help and all of a sudden I felt her presence in the room. There was a physical form in the room with me — sort of a light all around me. She whispered in my ear. She told me, 'Everything will be alright now.' It was like a thought form that was translated into Spanish." Carol says that following this visitation, she felt better and better. "Pretty soon I was able to handle the situa-

SIGNS AND SYMBOLS OF THE SECOND COMING

tion." In addition to the Virgin's appearance in the room, Carol is quick to point out that she felt others were "present" that were also helpful in making her get over this trying period.

REVEREND B.W. PALMER

Unfortunately, not many clergymen seem to be interested in these most recent manifestations of the Virgin Mary or other religious apparitions. Though they have acknowledged that such miracles have happened in the past, they seem hard-pressed to talk of such occurrences happening on a regular, day-to-day basis in our own time.

One exception is Reverend B.W. Palmer of Haines City, Florida, a Methodist clergyman. Reverend Palmer has devoted a good portion of his life in compiling hundreds of contemporary visions. In the book GODS OF AQUARIUS (Harcourt, Brace, and Jovanovich/Berkeley), my good friend Brad Steiger lists 24 of Reverend Palmer's observations on such manifestations, which he bases totally on those apparition cases that have been reported to him.

The list is as follows:

1. The heavens appear to open, and Mary, accompanied by angels, seems to descend.

2. Mary, Jesus, or a Holy Figure descends on a shaft of light into the presence of the percipient.

3. The Virgin appears or disappears through the solid wall of a room.

4. A percipient hears footsteps outside the house and a knock at the door. When he opens the door, he sees the Virgin Mary.

5. The form of the Virgin appears as if it were a picture on the wall.

6. The witness is awakened from his sleep by a sense of spirit presence, or by a touch, and sees the Holy Figure bending over him.

7. The apparition of an angel or a deceased person appears and leads the percipient to a place where the Holy Figure materializes.

8. The face of Jesus or the Virgin Mary manifests above a person who needs help or who needs to be comforted.

9. The percipient may hear a voice which tells him or her to go to a certain place and to do a certain thing. When the person does as the voice requests, he sees the Holy Figure.

10. The form of the Holy Figure is seen hugely manifested in the sky.

SIGNS AND SYMBOLS OF THE SECOND COMING

11. The percipient is awakened by the shining of a bright light in his room. When he opens his eyes, he sees the Holy Figure.

12. A cloud is seen moving toward a person. As it draws near, the form of a Holy Figure emerges. In other instances, the Holy Figure disappears into a cloud.

13. A cloud or mist forms within a room and a Holy Figure emerges.

14. The Holy Figure appears to several persons at the same time but is perceived differently by individuals in the group. By one, the Holy Figure may be seen as a flash of light; by another as a supernatural ball or cloud of light; by yet another, as an inner or external manifesting voice.

15. The Virgin Mary or other Holy Figure appears to one person while others in the room see other spirit beings, usually apparitions of the dead.

16. The Holy Figure appears in what are regarded as "supernatural" dreams because of miraculous healings or other special manifestations which occur in connection with the dreams.

17. The Holy Figure may disappear quickly; her form may fade gradually; she may walk away and disappear in the distance; she may pass through walls or doors which are closed; she may ascend through ceilings; or, she may ascend in a cloud.

18. In many vision stories, although the Holy Figure may not emerge from a "supernatural light," it is accompanied by a light which illuminates the area around the percipient. In some cases, the illumination may precede the appearance of the Holy Figure.

19. In most visions of the Virgin Mary, though the percipient(s) may see and speak to her, others present may be aware only of the percipient(s) talking to an unseen presence.

20. In several accounts, Jesus or the Virgin Mary is said to have manifested in a brilliant supernatural light which never takes on human form but from which may issue a voice, an influence, or a healing.

21. During an out-of-body experience, the witness sees the Virgin Mary or other Holy Figure, who was invisible to him during his normal in-body condition.

22. In other reports of out-of-body experiences, individuals state that they have traveled to distant places, such as the homes of friends and relatives, and viewed a Holy Figure.

23. During out-of-body experiences, men and women have claimed to have visited the lower spirit worlds or hells where they have viewed good spirits at-

SIGNS AND SYMBOLS OF THE SECOND COMING

tempting to help the lower spirits. In some instances during these lower-plane visits, they have reported seeing Jesus or the Virgin Mary.

24. Men and women who have been restored to life after a brief period of physical death have stated that they have seen Jesus and Mary in Heaven.

What Reverend Palmer neglected to mention is that many photos of these Holy Figures, such as the one below of Jesus, have been turning up from all over the world.

VALLIS, OREGON, THURSDAY, DECEMBER 24, 1964   Price 10 cents Per Copy

STRANGE CLOUD FORMATION

It has been almost a year since we first printed this picture, taken by a coast photographer just before sunset. Since that time we have had many requests that it be reprinted, but for a time we were unable to locate the film. We believe this photograph is one of the most remarkable ever taken, and feel that this week — just before Christmas — is an especially appropriate time to bring it to the attention of our readers. This unusual cloud formation, unexplainable though it be, brings encouragement that peace on earth and good will toward men may yet be attained.

Corvallis, Ore. newspaper,

SIGNS AND SYMBOLS OF THE SECOND COMING

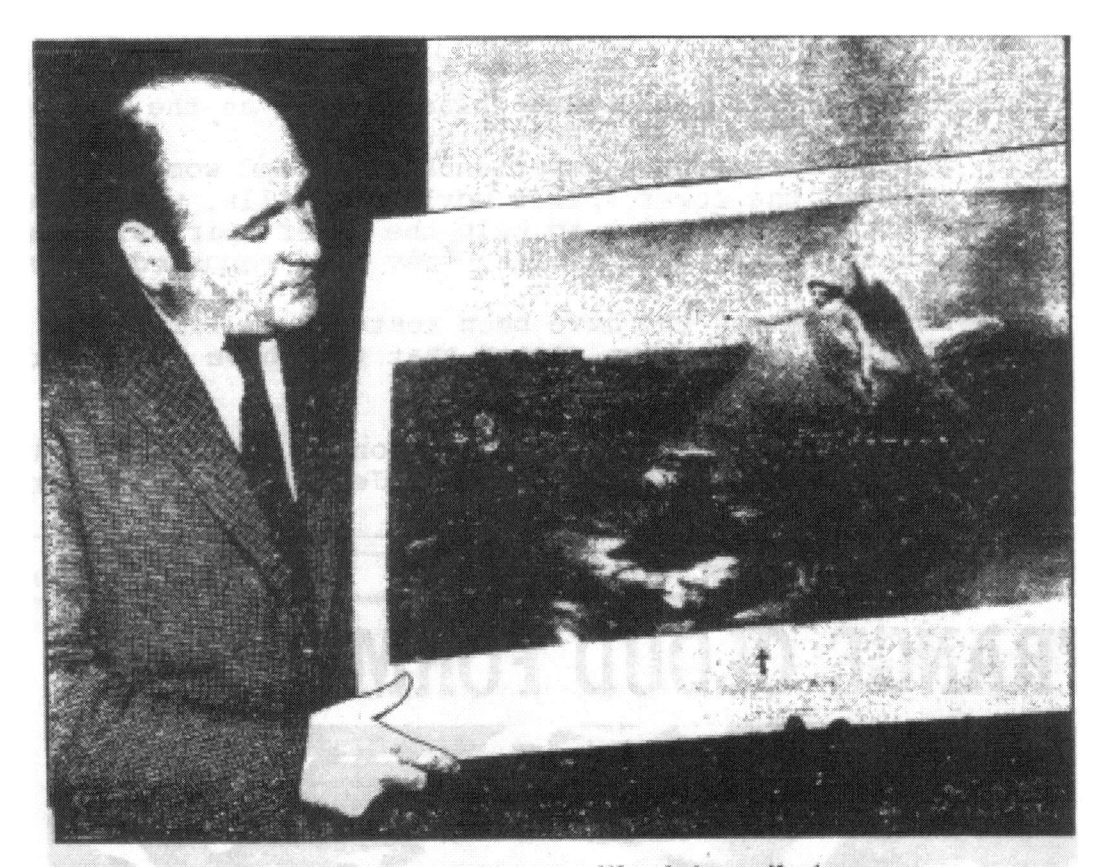

(Above) Richard Grave with picture that weeps.
(Below) Reproduction of 'Weeping Angel' picture.

SIGNS AND SYMBOLS OF THE SECOND COMING

THE WEEPING ANGEL

Richard Grave of Worthing, England, has in his possession a painting which shows an angel hovering above a Shepherd announcing the coming of Christ.

Mr. Grave found the old print in the garage next to the new home he had just purchased and was about to throw it away when a strange event transpired.

Here is what happened:

A Christ-like figure appeared in front of him, blocking his path. The figure said, "I AM HE," apparently meaning that he was Jesus. With his left hand, the vision reached out and touched the painting, which was in a glass frame. All at once, the glass on the picture shattered into bits and the mysterious figure is said to have disappeared in a blaze of orange light. Upon thrusting his left arm upward to protect his eyes from the flare-up, Grave suffered a burned left forearm and the angel picture was blackened and blistered.

A short time later, however, the print repaired itself, and has "wept" intermittently ever since. The figure in the vision has also returned many times. Grave told American writer Michael Barton the following story:

"It all started with those first glimpses then built up so that I could see and talk to a man I call the 'Master.' He is sparsely bearded, dressed in coarse robes with a red outer garment, and appears suddenly. When I can see him, he is as solid and real as the next man. It all began with the picture and so on. I thought I was going mad. So much has happened since, reports in which other people all over the country have proved for themselves that the 'Master' must be a real person with very real intentions that my peace of mind has returned."

One of the messages given to Richard Grave by this mysterious person was that "many and more substantial MANIFESTATIONS WILL FOLLOW so that the prophecy of my coming may remain kindled."

There are other cases of religious paintings shedding tears. There is, for example, a medieval painting owned by Mrs. Antonia Kulis of New York. The painting is of the Virgin Mary with the Christ Child in her arms. Tears are said to stream from the eyes of the Virgin Mary and sometimes will even drip onto the floor and form a small puddle. It is our understanding that when there is a bad catastrophe somewhere in the world, such as an earthquake or another disaster, the tears begin to form and drip for days with no scientific explanation.

SIGNS AND SYMBOLS OF THE SECOND COMING
CONCLUSION

With all of these manifestations increasing in number, it is obvious that there is a thinking intelligence behind such mysterious apparitions. Perhaps some big event is due which could change our lives and these are the signs and wonders that the Bible predicted. We welcome your comments and any additional information you might have. Address your correspondence to: Miracles, c/o Global Communications, PO Box 753, New Brunswick, NJ, 08903.

The signs that we speak of are all around us and they happen in such remarkable ways that they certainly do serve to help build our faith and show that God is NOT dead but is able to manifest in our crazy world of today.

Just before the outbreak of the Korean War, a missionary inside the People's Republic of China was fearful of his life and realized that he must soon leave the country. The people in his care were sad to see him go. The missionary was heartbroken and for a brief while began to doubt his faith. Just before he left, he got a mental impression to take a picture of a snow drift. When the picture was developed, he could clearly see the image of a Christ-like figure. The picture resembles many paintings of Jesus, with long hair, beard and a white robe.

This is a reproduction of the painting owned by Mrs. Antonia Kulis of New York. The image of the Virgin Mary cries whenever there is a disaster somewhere in the world. Scientists have looked the icon over and admit to being puzzled. Religious authorities are also hard pressed to explain this manifestation and say it could be a modern miracle.

SIGNS AND SYMBOLS OF THE SECOND COMING

SUGGESTED READING
AVAILABLE FROM THE PUBLISHER OR AMAZON.COM

**Project World Evacuation: UFOs to Assist in the
"Great Exodus" of Human Souls Off This Planet**
By Tuella and the Ashtar Command

UFOs, Prophecy and the End of Time
By Sean Casteel

Flying Saucers in the Holy Bible
By Reverend Virginia Brasington, Sean Casteel, Tim Swartz and G.C. Schellhorn

Angels of the Lord – Expanded Edition
By Timothy Green Beckley, Sean Casteel, Dr. Frank E. Stranges,
and William Alexander Oribello

The Excluded Books of the Bible
By Sean Casteel

SIGNS AND SYMBOLS OF THE SECOND COMING

Made in the USA
Middletown, DE
21 April 2016